Cornish Tales
(ancient and modern)

Cornwall Levant tin mine

A Cornish fishing-boat wreck on the rocks.

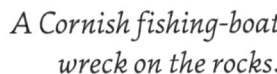

Florence Breed

Published in Australia by Sid Harta Publishers Pty Ltd,
ABN: 34 632 585 203
17 Coleman Parade, GLEN WAVERLEY VIC 3150 Australia
Telephone: +61 3 9560 9920, Facsimile: +61 3 9545 1742
E-mail: author@sidharta.com.au

First published in Australia 2020
This edition published 2020
Copyright © Florence Breed 2020
Cover design, typesetting: WorkingType (www.workingtype.com.au)

The right of Florence Breed to be identified as the Author of the Work has been asserted in accordance with the Copyright, Designs and Patents Act 1988.

The Author of this book accepts all responsibility for the contents and absolves any other person or persons involved in its production from any responsibility or liability where the contents are concerned.

All rights reserved. No part of this publication may be reproduced, stored in a retrieval system, or transmitted, in any form or by any means without the prior written permission of the publisher, nor be otherwise circulated in any form of binding or cover other than that in which it is published and without a similar condition being imposed on the subsequent purchaser.

Breed, Florence
Cornish Tales: ancient and modern
ISBN: 978-1-925707-07-6
pp380

See overleaf for detailed map of old Cornwall

iii

*Ruined engine houses.
A common sight in Cornwall.*

St. Gwinear, born in Ireland of Noble birth, came to Cornwall in the 5th. Century. He was beheaded by pagan chieftan Teudar at nearby Roseworthy, but was laid to peaceful rest here at Herland where the church now stands. The church was endowed by the Bishop of Exeter in 1311 A.D. but shows many traces of earlier Norman times. It is built mainly from local Elvan and granite.

Cornwall's Coat-Of-Arms (as seen on the cover) is composed of two figures, a Fisherman and a Miner, holding a shield with 15 round balls painted on it. On top of the shield stands a black Crow (the most common bird in Cornwall) and a crown represents the Duke of Cornwall. Most men in those olden days worked as miners — but fishermen were also essential because the staple food for poor Cornish folks used to be pilchards. The fifteen balls seen on the shield represent fifteen gold coins because during the time of the Crusades, the Earl of Cornwall was captured by the Saracens (Arabs) and he was only released after fifteen gold pieces were paid to his captors.

Old post office, Tintagel (near king Arthur's Castle)

CONTENTS

Preface	5
Introduction	9
Familiar Scenes In Cornwall	19
A Prehistoric Quoit — Tomb For The Dead	22
Punishments In Old Cornwall	26
A Fight To The Death	32
A Wife For Sale	35
Going, Going, Gone: When Auctioning A Wife!	41
The Cornish Giant	44
Cornwall — 16th.century	50
Accidents In The Mines	52
Two Old Headstones	55
Early Christian Monuments	68
Sheer Carelessness	71
The Death Of John Moyle (1799-1857)	73
Cornish Miners At Work	76
The Wheal Agar Lift Disaster	77
He Gave His Life To Save Another Man	80
Tin Miners	81
Captain Henry Skewes, 1812 — 1881	82
Stay In The Place Where You Were Born	86
Boiler Explosions	88
Fact Or Fiction	93
The Sermon On The Mount	96
Infant Tragedies	97
To Cornish Lads Who Fell In The Great War	99
England's Most Famous Sailor	100
Danger From Fire	103
From Crow-Scaring To Westminster	105
Helston's Ancient Customs	107
The Helston Floral Dance	110
At A Cornish Fair	112
Cock-Fighting	113
Bull-Baiting	116
Badger-Baiting	118
Facts Of 1500'S In Cornwall	120
The Stag	124
From Riches To Rags	128

The Knockers	133
The Copper Mines Of Camborne Supplied The World	137
The Cursing Psalm	140
Grave Words	145
Zennor — A Cornish Village	146
Detected By A Dream	152
The Ballad Of Mary Marten — Written By Her Murderer	154
Poisoning	155
The Wayward Hat	157
Transportation For Machine Breakers	162
Transportation For Burglary	168
The Cornish In America: John Skewes	171
Death Of A Cornishman In Nicaragua	174
Society And Superstition	178
The Worst Shipwreck In Cornish History	181
Social Conditions	185
A Son Of The Westcountry	190
Cornish Potato Cake	194
Survival At Sea	196
He Converted The Cornish Miners John Wesley (1703 — 1791)	201
John Wesley	203
John Wesley And The Methodists	205
Trewint	207
Rough Justice	212
The Cornish In Australia: A Fatal Mistake	216
Society	220
The Cornish Knew About It First	225
Shipwrecked!	229
Fishing In Cornwall	231
Cornish Myths	233
Children's Games Throughout The Centuries	236
The Last Hangings In England A Brutal Murder	239
The Cornish In South Australia	248
Death By Drowning At Morgan	250
Harry Moyle (1871-1888)	253
The Work Of A Royal Marine In WWI : A Cornishman	255
Food For The Old Cornish Folks	260
A Cornish Special	264

ix

Ginger Fairings	265
Potato Omelette	266
Cornish Stew	267
Soul Cakes	269
Captain Philip Gidley King	272
A Cornish Tragedy	274
A Crime Of Passion	277
Australia's First Free Farmer Was A Cornishman	280
The Bravest Convict Was A Cornishwoman	284
She Was The First — And The Last	291
A 'Titanic' Survivor Dies In Cornwall	296
R.m.s. Titanic, In Memoriam, April 15, 1912.	299
A Sad Letter From A Cornish Mother~	316
Cornish Memories Of An Evacuee	323
News From Cornwall	337
Heroism In New York — 2001	339
Old Cornwall And Its Miners	341
Sweat And Tears: A South Crofty Miner	343
A Cornish Poet: Charles Causley	345
Timothy Winters	346
Sir John Betjeman	347
Celebrating Cornwall's Mining History	348
A Child Of The Blitz	353
The Duchy Of Cornwall	365
Conclusion	367
Historical Facts Of Cornwall	369

Land's End

THE HURLERS – THREE STONE CIRCLES

Three bronze-age stone circles stand on Bodmin Moor (in North Cornwall) and originally the stones stood on granite paving. Over the years, many of these stones have disappeared so the circles are not as big as they once were. Tradition has it that they represent men who profaned the Lord's Day by playing the Cornish game of 'hurling' and so were turned into stones as a punishment.

Old Cornish Streets

THE HURLERS — THREE STONE CIRCLES

Scenes Of Looe

Saltash Brige
joins Cornwall to England
(opened 1859)

PREFACE

Were your ancestors Cornish miners? Then you may be interested in the following stories which describe life in Old Cornwall before that particular time when thousands of miners and their families were forced to emigrate after many of the mines closed down.

Were your ancestors tinners, or copperers? It does not matter which because both types of miners toiled hundreds of feet beneath the earth for meagre wages to make the mine owners rich.

My maternal grandfather worked in the Herland Mines (near Camborne) as a boy and then tried his luck as a young man in Salt Lake Valley, America. Later, he toiled in the cobalt mines of Canada.

I was familiar with parts of the far-west of Cornwall as a child attending the village school in St. Gwinear — and then I went to Truro to boarding school. In 1953, I began my teaching career in a little fishing-village by the name of Padstow, in North Cornwall. There were no boats in the harbour in those days because of the sand-bar.

Both my parents strongly spoke the Cornish dialect of their childhood, yet the last time I visited the old familiar places in 2003, I did not hear a genuine Cornish accent anywhere. It seems to me that foreigners have completely conquered Cornwall. They have bought and modernised those humble, miners' cottages, thus forcing house-prices up so high that the natives cannot afford to live in their own villages any longer.

The "Bad Old Days" may have gone and housework is easier, but whatever happened to those honest Cornish folks with their hard-working and generous ways?

*Boscastle Harbour
(c.1900)*

A Cornish Fisherman

Tin Miners

The Land of Saints   The Land of Pixies
The Land of Junket and Cream
Land of Tin   The Land of Widows
The Land of Giants

INTRODUCTION

Cornwall is cut off from the rest of England by the River Tamar which effectively makes the county an "island". Consequently, its geographical isolation meant that Cornish people developed their own language, food and customs — and regarded the rest of England as they would regard any other foreign country such as France, or Spain.

However, there was something particularly unusual which distinguished Cornwall from all other English counties — and that was its unique, immense, subterranean repository of copper and tin ores. Unfortunately there was no coal under Cornish soil.

For many centuries, even as far back as the time of the great Roman Empire, foreign ships arrived in Cornwall to take away its tin. There is an ancient legend (concerning the "Hidden Years" of Christ's boyhood) which says that Jesus actually visited Cornwall with his uncle who was the wealthy merchant named Joseph of Arimathea. The hymn writer asks that very same question in his lines from "Jerusalem":

> "And did those feet in ancient times walk upon England's mountains green? And was the Holy Lamb of God on England's pleasant pastures seen?"

Jews came to Cornwall to trade for the precious metal and that is why smelting-houses near the tin mines were known locally as "Jews' Houses", even up to the 19th century.

A small village on the coast near Penzance bears the Jewish name of MARAZION (meaning "Bitter Heaven"). The origin of its name goes back to ancient times when a merchant ship struck the rocks nearby and many Jews were drowned. Their bodies were washed ashore and buried in that place.

Shipwreck

Cornwall was well-known to the Medes, Persians, Phoenicians and Greeks who all came to buy "the white metal that did not rust".

My ancestors were Cornish, except for my maternal grandmother, Selina Coat. She was a "furriner" from North Devon who met my grandfather when he was staying with his sister in Swansea. Grandfather Sampson was a miner, like all the rest of my ancestors who were born in this land of tin.

Mines and mining played a big part in my ancestors' lives, as the reader will see, for they all lived in mining villages where stacks and buildings dominated the horizon for miles around. This was their world in which they lived and worked.

The mine owners boasted of untold riches stretching down into the bowels of the earth, but it was the miners, such as my ancestors, who had to risk life and limb working one thousand, two thousand, three thousand feet down below in a labyrinth of dark, steamy tunnels to obtain this treasure. Yet the miner was very poorly-paid, and if he survived all the hazards of mining he died young anyway, from dust on his lungs.

As for the Cornish women — many would be a widow by the age of 40, left with a large family to care for, yet knowing that all her sons would follow in their father's footsteps "into the mine" .... for that was their destiny.

Until the beginning of the nineteenth century miners were able to use local timber to smelt the tin, but when trees became scarce the mine owners were forced to import large quantities of coal from Wales to fuel their smelting houses. No wonder the environment was bare and without shelter from the elements.

Miners built their own houses, simple structures made of stones — that cost nothing, but the toil of carrying them from nearby waste land.

A Stone House

*Without pilchards and potatoes
the Cornish would have starved*

A FISHERWOMAN OF ST. IVES (c. 1800)

INTRODUCTION

VICTIMS OF THE CORNISH WRECKERS

Of course, most miners built their humble stone houses close to the mines where they were employed and so avoided the extra hardship of having to walk a great distance after their daily shift. Cornwall's climate is a harsh one — plenty of rain, fog and gales, and bitterly cold for most months of the year — so shelter from the cruel elements needs to be easily available. However, there was not enough space for all miners to live close by their mine shafts.

My mining ancestors were poor in spite of the fact that by the middle of the 18th century the mines of Cornwall were producing three quarters of all the copper used in the world and nearly half the tin. To procure this wealth, hundreds of miles of shafts were sunk and thousands of miles of tunnels were driven and forests of timber were used to support the ground, whilst mountains of ore and rivers of water had to be brought to the surface.

But it was the mine owner who was rich, not the Cornish miner such as my grandfather (Stephen Sampson), or my great-grandfather (Henry Skewes), or my great-great-grandfather (Thomas Moyle). Although skilled workmen they remained poor because they were not paid a wage; they worked under an unfair system (tribute) which paid so many shillings according to the ore sent up to the surface. Thus, their wages depended on the richness of the vein (lode) so sometimes they might earn nothing at all.

Was it a healthy job, working stripped to the waist with sweat streaming down their faces and bodies in temperatures of 115 degrees Fahrenheit, the air so bad a candle could scarcely burn? As there was no compulsory, free education in those days my grandfather started working underground when he was ten and he said the worst part of the job was climbing up and down perpendicular ladders. Many miners fell from the slippery rungs to their death.

In order to learn about our Cornish ancestors, it is absolutely essential to understand their unique environment with its ancient history so that one can place them within a meaningful context. Let me begin, dear reader, with a few facts about this land of my people.

It is written that in the year 1377 after a "fearful plague" had raged throughout the land, the inhabitants of Cornwall numbered only 34,960. However, by the year 1775 when my great-great-grandfather Thomas Moyle was born, there would have been nearer 300,000.

A writer once described Cornwall as "one of the more ancient, celebrated and romantic portions of the British Isles". Certainly it was the most isolated and primitive (even the Romans left it alone) and the last wolf in England was killed here, in the Parish of Ludgvan.

The Cornish had spoken their own language for centuries. Even when the writer was a child, there were still many words spoken by Cornish folk that "foreigners from across the Tamar" could not understand.

Once famous for its mineral resources unequalled in the world, the Cornishmen have been miners of tin from time immemorial — and later they also mined copper.

Cornwall is remarkable for its geographical position, hence its nickname "The Toe-Cap of England". The ancient Latin name for Cornwall was "Cornubia" which accurately describes its figure (shaped like a cornucopia, or horn of plenty).

The length of this county is no more than 80 miles; and its widest part is just 45 miles which diminishes gradually until, as it nears Land's End, the distance from coast to coast is only about 6 miles.

Cornwall's rocky coasts, grassy headlands, fertile valleys and granite peaks are constantly lashed by the restless waves of the Atlantic Ocean. Strong sea-gales bring lashing rains, which makes the climate a very damp one, though mild. This kind of weather contributed greatly to the spread of rheumatism and tuberculosis that was once the curse of the old Cornish folk.

It is a fact that sometime during his reign (1509-1547) King Henry VIII visited Cornwall to inspect its greatest tin works which were situated at Hayle; and this surely proves the economic importance of Cornwall, even during this particular king's turbulent life-time.

During the reign of Queen Elizabeth 1 when Spain was England's greatest enemy, the Cornish suffered greatly from the Spaniards who had a nasty habit of attacking and ransacking the coastal villages.

The worst invasion occurred in July, 1595, when Spanish ships sailed into Mount's Bay carrying soldiers. These Spaniards landed and ravished the three fishing villages of Mousehole, Paul and Newlyn, systematically looting and burning each house to the ground.

It is said that the inhabitants offered no resistance to the enemy because of an old superstition which foretold their catastrophe.

The Cornwall that is familiar to modern tourists is certainly not the Cornwall of my childhood, for that was still

a land of ancient traditions, superstitions and customs. Nothing significantly changed until after the Second World War when the availability and popularity of motor vehicles brought to an end the isolation of its tiny hamlets and villages.

By the mid- 1950's, electricity cables and water pipes had reached even the remotest areas and Cornwall was dragged into the 20th. Century at last.

Alas, the Cornwall that I once knew bears little resemblance to the tourist-Mecca which is Cornwall today.

FAMILIAR SCENES IN CORNWALL

Cornish Tales

Today, many tourists visit the quaint little town of St. Germans — it is only ten miles from Plymouth after crossing the River Tamar into Cornwall — a quaint little place consisting of one main street with picturesque cottages situated in the pretty valley of the River Lynher; however, St. German is famous for its ancient Norman church.

It is the church's west front with two towers and a magnificent doorway of pure Norman work which attracts the visitor's attention. The archway over the door consists of seven rings of carved, grey-green stonework, making it "the noblest portal in all England".

Standing before it, one is overwhelmed by the grandeur of its design and the unique workmanship of those 12th. Century stonemasons. For seven hundred years this noble portal has been exposed to the relentless fury of wind and rain, yet even in its weather-worn condition such glory is undimmed. This church contains a memorial to Sir John MOYLE, of Bake.

ST. GERMAN'S

A prehistoric QUOIT – tomb for the dead

THE MOST FAMOUS CORNISH CHURCH
St. Germans Church (Late Norman)

The church of St. Germans stands at the end of the town, which today is little more than a village with its one street built on the slope of a wooded valley. Tradition says that the bishopric of Cornwall had its seat here as early as 614. There was a college of priests founded here by King Athelstan that later became an Augustinian priory. The present church dates from about 1150. Its chancel was destroyed by fire in 1592. Parts of the church are beautifully-decorated in the English style, but its outstanding feature is the fine Norman doorway with two towers, originally octagonal (see picture). Close to the venerable church stands a stately manor-house once owned by the bishop and the monks, but now belonging to Earl St. Germans.

Cornish Tales

RIVER TAMAR

BRUNEL RAILWAY BRIDGE (1859)
and ROAD BRIDGE (1961)

THE LIZARD

THE MOST FAMOUS CORNISH CHURCH St. Germans Chunch (Late Norman)

By 'tre'-, 'pol'-, and 'pen'- you shall know the Cornish men

PUNISHMENTS IN OLD CORNWALL

Even up to the end of the eighteenth century public whippings were still very common as a severe punishment for stealing anything from oats to milk. It was intended as a deterrent to stop other thieves, yet to modern folks the severe punishment may seem much worse than the crime they had committed.

Even people who committed trivial offences were often flogged through the streets till the blood ran down their backs. Men could be put to death for stealing a sheep, or a watch — and lunatics were shut up in cages and scoffed, poked and jeered at by passers-by.

In 1813, Eliza Osborne was accused of setting fire to a cornfield and subsequently hanged. That same year a poor farm labourer, William Wallis, was sentenced to death for stealing and killing a sheep to feed his large family. An unemployed youth named James Northey was found guilty of housebreaking and robbery and sentenced to death.

Needless to say, capital punishment was inevitably the fate of a murderer. For example, there was William Burns who killed his fellow signalman in a fight at the Land's End lighthouse-station; he was hanged at Bodmin on the 1st. April, 1814.

In those days hangings took place in public. They were performed in full view of people, who obviously enjoyed the thrilling spectacle and regarded hangings as a form of live entertainment. People of all ages would flock to watch the death-throes of a condemned person and almost considered it their solemn duty to bear witness to such punishments.

Cornwall's last public hanging took place in August, 1862, at Bodmin. Here, on a sloping field so that the scaffold was in full view of the thousands of spectators, John Doidge, aged 28, of Launceston, was hanged. He had lost his job to a man called Roger Drewe and therefore he murdered Drewe because he blamed him for his misfortune. Doidge was hanged by Calcraft, a well-known and expert hangman.

Early that morning, two women came to the gates of the gaol pleading to be allowed near the prisoner after his hanging because they believed that his dead hand if laid upon their sore necks would cure them. The hand must still be warm — and this was a popular superstition because a long queue of sick folks would often be seen waiting for a dead man's touch.

There are many things which shock us when we come to know more of what life was like in Cornwall two hundred or more years ago. As stated previously, the punishment for people who had committed even a trivial offence, was a sound whipping in the streets for all to witness.

In October, 1811, James Barnes was found guilty of stealing oats and immediately sentenced to be publicly whipped on the following Saturday.

In 1878, there was a flogging at Bodmin Gaol when Joseph Trewartha, a miner, was convicted for assaulting another miner, John Taylor, and stealing his gold watch. Trewartha was sentenced to ten months imprisonment and twenty-five lashes of the cat-o'-nine-tails. This is a particularly vicious kind of whip consisting of nine kotted cords fastened to a handle — and so called because it leaves marks like the scratches of a cat.

The prisoner, Joseph Trewartha, received his lashes in the main corridor of the gaol so that his cries and groans of pain might be clearly heard by other prisoners over a long distance. It was believed that such a punishment could serve as a suitable deterrent to him and to others for a long time to come.

At Bodmin Assizes in April, 1835, three men were transported to Australia for life because they stole two bullocks belonging to a Farmer W. Blake. Their names were Henry Symons, his brother Samuel Symons and an associate, Thomas Kendall.

Also transported for life was Charles Mansell for stealing hay belonging to a Farmer J. Carne.

For stealing candles from the mine where they worked, John Deeble and Matthew Dawson were imprisoned for one month with hard labour, but first they were publicly whipped in front of their fellow-workers at the mine, presumably, to deter other miners from stealing candles at work.

In April, 1867, two sailors from a French ship that was docked in Falmouth harbour, were summoned to appear at Penryn Police Court charged with stealing a favourite pet cat belonging to John Tregellas.

The two French sailors pleaded guilty and were sent to prison for seven days. However, there was some amusement in the courtroom when the sailors, having been ordered to return the cat to its owner, had to confess that the stolen animal had already been skinned, dressed and made ready for the barbecue.

Four young boys were sentenced to flogging at Bodmin in January, 1868, for breaking into a brewery and stealing a barrel of beer. These four juvenile culprits were certainly not spared the cat-o'-nine-tails because of their youth as Guest and Bailey each received twelve lashes, whilst Trelease and Downing had nine lashes each.

In January, 1862, a young man was sentenced to transportation for life after he confessed to being a body-snatcher. It seems he had been one of six men who had exhumed the body of a young woman from a newly-dug grave in St. Ives churchyard. He said that he and his five mates were paid 12 pounds (2 pounds each) by a medical man who required the body for anatomical purposes.

In April, 1864, a French vessel put into Falmouth harbour to shelter from severe gales in the English Channel. Two French seamen belonging to this vessel took advantage of their stay in the harbour to go ashore and gather a basket of snails in order to enjoy a feast.

However, in the course of their search for such delicacies, the Frenchmen saw a pheasant's nest on Sir Samuel Spry's estate and helped themselves to the eggs. Unfortunately, they were caught by the strangulation and then concealed, or just left to die, in some hidden ditch where its cries could not be heard. Desperate women were forced to use desperate measures in those days before the welfare state was created.

At the Redruth Assizes in August, 1871, many people showed interest in the punishment meted out to a woman called Libby who was charged with murdering and mutilating her infant child. A sentence of penal servitude for ten years was passed upon her. Her severe punishment was regarded with satisfaction by the local inhabitants since Redruth had become notorious for the destruction of new-born infants.

Another kind of common punishment was the use of public-stocks. For example, in May, 1862, Nathaniel Cole was placed in the stocks for six hours because he did not not pay a fine of ten shillings which had been inflicted upon him for being drunk and disorderly — and for his riotous behaviour.

Likewise, on the same day at Hayle, James Bawden, of St. Erth, was placed in the stocks in Foundry Square for being drunk and not paying the fine. (The last recorded use of stocks in Cornwall was at Camborne in 1866.)

One should remember that the vice of drunkenness was common almost all classes of people in those early days and the old saying *"as drunk as a lord"* shows that it was not just confined to the working classes.

Heavy drinking was perhaps more prevalent in Cornwall than in other parts of England owing to the smuggling trade around the Cornish coast. This enabled brandy and other spirits to be brought over from France in huge quantities and at such low prices that even the poorest folks could afford them.

When the wreck of a ship laden with wine or spirits occurred, people would flock to the shore and rescue the floating casks of liquor to take home. Or they would drink it on the spot and consequently get so drunk that they fell into the sea and were drowned. Such drinking caused a vast amount of misery and frequently led to fighting, murder and other crimes.

The Cornish had inherited fierce characteristics from their Celtic forefathers and were always ready to settle any differences with their fists. In 1864 a case came before the Penryn Courts when a prisoner, Edgar Retalick, was accused of causing grievous bodily harm to a shoemaker by the name of William Cock.

Apparently, the two men had been drinking together in the Bugle Inn when they started an argument that deteriorated into a fight. *"We had some strong words and he struck me,"* said William Cock, *"and when I caught hold of him fast so he could not strike me again, he bit off my ear."*

To support the seriousness of the matter, a policeman produced the ear wrapped in a piece of paper as evidence — and Cock looked at it and identified it as belonging to him.

In his own defence the prisoner said, "Cock assaulted me first and when he caught me around the neck I thought he intended to choke me to death so I fastened my teeth into the nearest part of him. I didn't mean to bite it right off."

Retalick was sent to prison for several months; whereas Cock had to spend the rest of his life with only one ear.

If the Cornish had a fault, it was their keenness for a fight. For example, in 1860 two miners by the names of Richard Piper and John Bodiner, had for some months previously been on unfriendly terms.

Saturday was 'Pay-Day' for miners and so these two men happened to meet each other in 'The Rising Sun' at Calstock. There were numerous miners assembled who witnessed the angry words that took place between Piper and Bodiner.

The two miners were determined to fight each other, but the publican naturally told them to leave his premises so they adjourned to a neighbouring field followed by about 200 individuals.

A FIGHT TO THE DEATH

In the centre of a circle, formed by the two hundred or more eager onlookers, Piper and Bodiner practised pugilism with such fierce, fast blows that even the watchers were dazed and sickened by the rivers of blood that poured freely from the noses and mouths of both men.

After two hours of fighting without a break, Bodiner received a fatal blow from Piper to the side of his head and collapsed upon the ground in a battered, bloody heap.

He only survived for a few moments and ceased breathing long before the doctor arrived on the scene.

The man who dealt that final, fatal blow was also fearfully mangled; his face was a spectacle to behold and his right eye was completely blind. The left eye had very little sight left in it and so, for the rest of his life, Piper was an invalid, unable to work again to support his wife and children. Henceforth, blindness and poverty would be his constant companions.

The local magistrate did not see fit to punish the winner in that duel to the death as both men had willingly participated in the fight so it could scarcely be termed "murder" — and, anyway, he thought that Piper had received sufficient punishment for the part he played in Bodiner's death.

A FIGHT TO THE DEATH

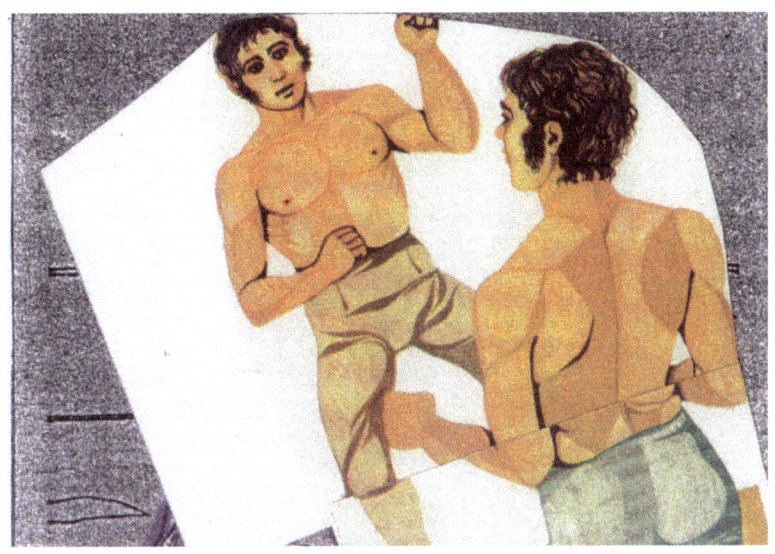

BARE-KNUCKLE FIGHTING
The Cornish took the sport of bare-knuckle fighting everywhere they went.

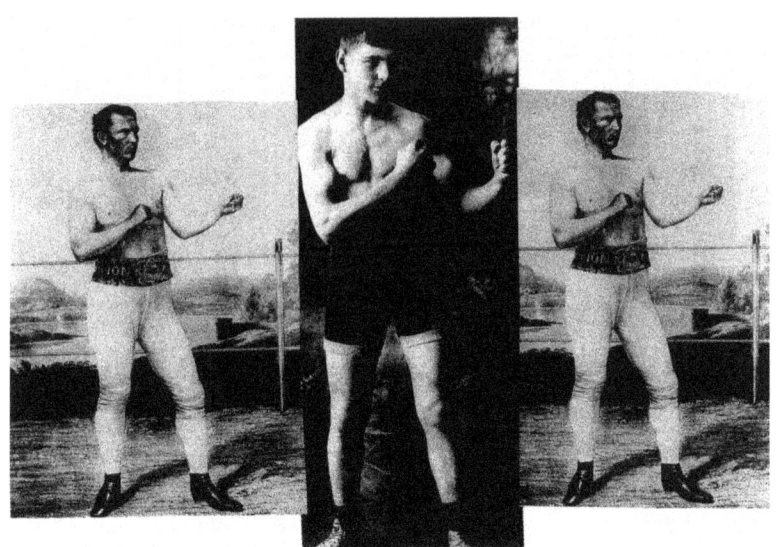

Bare-Knuckle Fighting in Cornwall

A WIFE FOR SALE

An ancient parish church stands in the centre of St. Austell and is famous for its unique Saxon communion cup that was found on the outskirts of the town by miners in the year 1774 when they were digging a deep shaft.

About two miles north of this large, bustling, market-town stands Hensbarrow Hill, one of the loftiest heights in Cornwall, whilst nearby in Pentuan Vale are rich quarries that supply wonderful marble used in the construction of many churches and stately mansions throughout this ancient county.

In particular, about three miles outside St. Austell at Menacuddle Hill there is a holy well next to the remains of an ancient chapel and a waterfall. The well is believed to have been blessed by none other than Saint Austell himself.

Now, there is a true event connected with this quaint old Cornish town that took place one Friday in summer during the year 1835.

It concerns a man and a woman who were seen approaching the town on foot, making their way towards the market-place.

However, before climbing a very steep hill to reach the high plain on which St. Austell stands, these two strangers first crossed a long and dreary tract of abandoned tin-mines where the ground is strewn with broken bricks and prickly gorse bushes.

The man walks with the slow, heavy gait of a farm labourer, his swarthy face almost hidden by an unkempt, bushy beard, whilst the woman, who appears to be much younger than the man, plods silently behind him, her pretty face just visible beneath a faded, crumpled bonnet. Black ringlets reach almost down to her waist and her shoes are down-trodden and dusty.

Arriving at the top of the hill, this ill-matched pair continue their weary way over the cobbled pavements, passing pleasant-looking villas before entering the narrow streets of the town. These dirty, dingy lanes possess a somewhat gloomy appearance, but further along in the main street there are some interesting buildings such as the grand-looking Town Hall built from local granite and marble.

They trudge past the huge Devon and Cornwall Bank and the long terrace of alms-houses — until they reach the work-house and then the stannary-hall and several noisy drinking-places. At last, they arrive in the busy market-square where hundreds of horses and cows have already been sold that morning, so now there are only a few inferior animals left standing in isolated pens dotted around the square.

The crowd is denser near the tables of the fruit and vegetable vendors. Women, waiting patiently outside the tent of the fortune-teller, suddenly notice the two strangers and begin to stare at them.

Indeed, the local inhabitants must have been very surprised by the appearance of a man of somewhat advanced age leading a woman of about thirty by a halter which is tied around her waist.

The fellow's name is George Trethewey, a farm labourer residing in the parish of St. Stephen's, who having become tired of his wife had adopted his own peculiar method of disposing of her as if she were a common farm animal, He decided to put her up for sale in the market at St. Austell.

Trethewey continued his slow amble across the town-square, intending to sell his wife to the highest bidder. Surprisingly, the poor woman does not seem the slightest bit perturbed and appears rather indifferent to the whole proceedings.

The husband pushes his way through the crowds towards a canvas tent marked, 'Home-Brewed Beer, Ale and Cyder'. He continued to unceremoniously drag the woman behind him, regardless of her discomfort at having to endure the rough, leather halter around her thin waist.

Inside the drinking-tent he bought himself a pot of beer, but ignored the woman's thirst because he intended to rid himself of her very soon anyway.

The inquisitive stares of other drinkers in the tent eventually made him feel uncomfortable, but still holding tightly to the woman's halter he announced in a loud voice, *"I don't see why men who have got wives and don't want them, shouldn't sell them just as farmers sell unwanted cows."*

The listeners nearest to him looked shocked at such a queer announcement, but he continued to speak in a rough, uncouth manner. *"So, I am open to any bid for this wonderful piece of creation. Will anybody buy her?"*

At first there was a deathly silence in the tent after such a strange question, but then the listeners thought it was only a joke and everyone began to laugh at him.

Then above the noise of the crowd Trethewey continued to speak. "Doesn't anybody want this gem? She'll make a pretty bird for someone."

The people in the beer tent began to laugh even louder at such nonsense, regarding the stranger with mirth, thinking his words were just the inane prattlings of a drunkard.

"Won't anyone amongst you buy my goods? I am open to

any offer," continued the husband. "This woman is no good to me. Who'll have her?"

The people in the beer tent became quiet when they realised this man was in earnest about selling his wife and some of the women began to synpathise with the poor creature by calling her husband *"a cruel monster"* and *"an unfeeling devil"*.

Now amongst the huge crowd of spectators were two itinerant tinkers who travelled around Cornwall together, visiting scattered hamlets and villages to mend pots and pans. They both seemed very interested in the woman and one of them offered twopence for his wife.

"Twopence," growled the husband, *"I want more than that for such a perfect piece of womanhood,"* So, after a short consultation, the tinker's companion doubled the sum, explaining to the husband that they were acting in partnership and wanted to share her.

"It's all very well to agree to buy her, but first put down your money so as I know you mean it," *growled Trethewey*.

One of the tinkers immediately stepped forward and held out some coins in his hand. The husband looked at the proffered coins and quickly agreed to accept their offer, so the two tinkers handed over fourpence to him.

Trethewey hastily removed the halter from around his wife's waist without so much as a glance at her face, if he had bothered to look into her eyes he would have seen the bitter hatred and contempt that she felt for him — and just before he picked up the money, his wife with all the force she could summon spat into his ugly, bushy face.

Thus the woman was delivered to her two purchasers with whom she quite happily left the tent and proceeded to the nearest ale-house where the three of them regaled themselves with a jug of cider and happily drank to each other's health.

No doubt she thought any man who wanted her would be far better company than her miserable, mean, old husband.

Meanwhile the satisfied husband was about to depart with his money and very pleased that he had rid himself of such an expensive burden when the collector of market-tolls stopped him and demanded a penny which was the exact sum usually paid by a farmer for selling his pig, or cow, in the market-place.

"That's cheap at the price," mumbled Trethewey and paid the toll-collector a penny. He then proceeded homewards, apparently well-satisfied at ridding himself of a wife.

A happy bachelor

"Where I come from, men still sell their wives because the poor can't afford a divorce, you see, but if everyone agrees, then the woman can be sold. But it has to be done in the market-place. You put a rope around her neck, or waist, lead her there and offer her to the highest bidder. Among the people I come from, such a divorce is as good as an Act of Parliament. The lawyers and the Church don't reckon it is, but who cares a fig about what those greedy bastards think?" said one man who wanted to sell his wife.

In 1827, a young wife was sold at a Yorkshire beer-shop

because her husband said she had an idle nature — although instead of an halter he led her along by a piece of pink ribbon which was an unusual sign of kindness.

In 1837 a law was passed that made it a criminal offence for a man to advertise his wife for sale — and the punishment if he did so, was two months' imprisonment. But in spite of this law, in 1842 a farmer in Carlisle sold his wife of only three years for the remarkably high price of twenty guineas — and a Newfoundland dog. Although this wife selling custom declined in the 19th. Century, yet in 1859 there was a case where a wife changed hands for only a pint of ale — and in 1887, in Leicester a mason sold his wife to a blacksmith for four shillings. As late as 1930, a wife was sold at Bilston, in Staffordshire, but her price was not revealed.

He sold his wife for four pennies

The last recorded sale of a wife in Cornwall took place in January, 1846, when a man sold his wife to a farmer in the open market at Callington for the princely sum of two shillings and sixpence. Apparently, neither the authorities, nor any member of the public stepped forward to prevent such a barbaric and outlawed practice.

"WIVES AND WIND ARE NECESSARY EVILS", IS AN OLD SAYING — YET DOES THAT EXCUSE MEN FOR TREATING WOMEN AS INFERIOR BEINGS?

GOING, GOING, GONE
WHEN AUCTIONING A WIFE!

Cornwall was not the only county in England with that strange custom of selling wives. In fact, selling a wife was an accepted practice among all the English lower working-classes because it was a common idea that a wife was merely a chattel to be bought, or sold, at her husband's whim.

However, to keep the matter legal three things were necessary — (a) the sale had to be carried out in a public place such as in a cattle market, and, (b) it was necessary for the woman to have a leather halter around her neck, and, (c) she must not be sold for less than sixpence.

So, here are some examples from other parts of England to prove that the Cornish were not alone in practising this ancient custom. In 1802, in Derbyshire, a wife, together with a houseful of furniture, were sold for only 11 shillings. In that same year, a farmer in Devon sold his wife to another farmer for 'three cows and a steer', but no money changed hands.

In 1806, in Halifax, Yorkshire, a man married a widow whose soldier husband was presumed killed, but some years later the missing soldier husband returned and demanded his wife back. After heated negotiations the soldier husband agreed to sell his wife to the second husband for six shillings — and delivered her to him with a halter around her neck.

In 1812, a farrier sold his wife at a busy cattle market in a Dorset town. Although she did not generate much enthusiasm while being led by the leather halter around the cattle ring, she was eventually sold for sixpence.

In 1813, a butcher sold is wife by public auction at a market in Hereford for the respectable sum of 25 shillings — and a bowl of punch.

In 1818, in Little Horton, Yorkshire, a wife was sold in an auction room because now people had started to believe in the power of advertising rather than using local cattle markets. But by the 1820's men were beginning to find it difficult to sell their wives as customs were changing — and auctioneers began refusing to sell a man's wife for him.

In 1827, a young wife was sold at a Yorkshire beer shop because her husband said she had an idle nature — although instead of a halter he led her along by a pink ribbon which was an unusual sign of kindness.

In 1837 a law was passed that made it a criminal offence for a man to advertise his wife for sale — and the punishment if he did so was two months' imprisonment. But in spite of this law, in 1842 a farmer in Carlisle sold his wife of only three years for the remarkably high price of twenty guineas — and a Newfoundland dog.

- Although this wife-selling custom declined in the 19th. Century, yet in 1859 there was a case when a wife changed hands for only a pint of ale — and in 1887, in Leicester, a mason sold his wife to a blacksmith for 4s. As late as 1930 a wife was sold at Bilston, in Staffordshire, but her price was not revealed.

A Cattle Market

THE CORNISH GIANT

By the age of 21 Anthony Payne already stood 7ft. 4ins. tall so his father (a tenant-farmer at Stratton in the north of Cornwall) thought he would send him to be a servant in the household of Sir Beville Granville, of Stowe House. The young man proved to be a loyal and hard-working employee and even grew another two inches while in Sir Granville's service.

In spite of his great height and bulk, Payne was regarded as a witty and intelligent man who showed no signs of clumsiness, impressing everyone who knew him with his dexterity and quick reflexes. His fellow-workers said he had the brains to match the brawn — which made him a truly 'mighty giant'.

Witnesses tell an amazing story about Payne's great strength. It seems that one chilly Christmas Eve a boy from the kitchen was sent into the woods to fetch logs for the great fire in the hall. The boy took a donkey with him to carry the load of wood, but both got lost in the snow. Payne was sent to find them and when he saw the lad almost frozen to death, to save time he carried the loaded donkey on his shoulders and the boy in his arms.

When civil war erupted between Parliament and King Charles 1, in 1642, Cornwall stood on the side of the king.

Before long a large battalion of 'Roundheads' (the nickname for followers of Oliver Cromwell) crossed the River Tamar into Cornwall and camped on top of a steep hill just outside Stratton village. It looked very bad for the Cornishmen. This Parliamentarian force was under the command of the Earl of Stamford and consisted of 5,400 infantrymen, 200 cavalry, 13 cannons and a great mortar gun.

*the Cornish Giant
Anthony Payne
(7'-4")*

Facing Stamford and his large army were Sir Ralph Hotpoint and Sir Beville Granville with less than 3,000 men. Bravely they decided that "come what may" they must attack the enemy in their camp on a steep hill. Payne stayed close to his master, acting as Sir Granville's bodyguard and no doubt the opposing soldiers were terrified when they saw this giant advancing towards them — no one would have dared to fight him.

Battle commenced on Tuesday, 16th. May, at dawn, when the Cornish Royalists moved up the hill to attack. The pikemen (nicknamed 'hedgehogs') led the way with fire support from their Musketeers and Light Artillery. The fight lasted for ten hours by which time the Cornish had used up all their ammunition; so as a last show of courage they decided to put their trust in 'cold steel'. Led by the giant Payne, they marched forward in silence, steel swords raised high, glinting ominously in the sunshine and blinding the enemy.

The thought of cold steel was too much for the nerves of the Roundheads who retreated in terror and soon disappeared from sight, leaving their dead and wounded strewn across the battlefield.

The giant Payne was put in charge of burying the dead, so he told his men to dig trenches large enough to hold ten bodies each. Nine bodies lay side by side in the first trench, but as Payne approached carrying the tenth body and was about to lay him in the trench, the man spoke. "Surely you wouldn't bury me, Mr. Payne, before I am dead?" pleaded the Roundhead.

Effortlessly holding the body in the crook of his huge arm, Payne calmly replied, "I tell thee, man, our trench was dug to hold ten men. At the moment there's only nine in it, so you must take your place."

"But I'm not dead," pleaded the man, "I haven't done living yet. Be merciful, Mr. Payne, don't hurry a poor fellow into the earth before his time."

"I don't wish to hurry you," Payne answered, "I just mean to put you down gently and cover you up and then you can die at your leisure." The poor soldier must have been terrified at the thought of being buried alive, but the gentle giant was only teasing him; and after the burial task was completed, Payne carried his wounded enemy home to his cottage and cared for him.

OLIVER CROMWELL
'Lord Protector' of the Commonwealth

Cornwall never again had to face Cromwell's armies; no doubt due to the fact that throughout history the River Tamar has always been a natural defence and few enemies ever bothered to cross it. Even the Ancient Romans only marched west as far as Exeter after landing on the south coast of Britain.

In the north of England the Royalist cause was lost and eventually in 1646 King Charles 1 surrendered after losing the battle of Naseby, in Northamptonshire.

Oliver Cromwell and Parliament now took charge of the country and the king was executed in 1649. Thus, the country became a Republic and no man in England had more power than Cromwell who ruled with an iron fist. When he died in 1658 the people felt free to call back to the throne the son of Charles I and in 1660 Charles II was crowned — and Britain never wanted to be a Republic again.

THE CROMWELL WAY

HISTORY provides a lesson in how to deal with a Parliament seen as corrupt and finished. In 1653, Oliver Cromwell lost patience with the House after learning that it was attempting to stay in session despite an agreement to dissolve.

His speech will still resonate today with disgusted voters. This is what he said:

'It is high time for me to put an end to your sitting in this place, which you have dishonoured by your contempt of all virtue, and defiled by your practice of every vice; ye are a factious crew, and enemies to all good government; ye are a pack of mercenary wretches, and would like Esau sell your country for a mess of pottage, and like Judas betray your God for a few pieces of money.

Is there a single virtue now remaining amongst you? Is there one vice you do not possess? Ye have no more religion than my horse; gold is your God; which of you have not barter'd your conscience for bribes? Is there a man amongst you that has the least care for the good of the Commonwealth?

Ye sordid prostitutes have you not defil'd this sacred place, and turn'd the Lord's temple into a den of thieves, by your immoral principles and wicked practices? Ye are grown intolerably odious to the whole nation; you were deputed here by the people to get grievances redress'd, are yourselves become the greatest grievance.

Your country therefore calls upon me to cleanse this Augean stable, by putting a final period to your iniquitous proceedings in this House; and which by God's help, and the strength he has given me, I am now come to do; I command ye therefore, upon the peril of your lives, to depart immediately out of this place; go, get you out!

Make haste! Ye venal slaves be gone! So! Take away that shining bauble there, and lock up the doors. In the name of God, go!'

Oliver Cromwell

Trial of KING CHARLES I

They say that King Charles II's successful reign was not so much in what he did, but rather in what he refrained from doing.

After the Restoration of the Monarchy King Charles II appointed Sir John Saville as Governor of the Plymouth Garrison and Anthony Payne became Sir John's halberdier — that is a man who protects his master by carrying a long spear which has a battle-axe on the end (in modern times it would be like carrying a gun for protection).

The king often visited Sir John and liked the friendly giant so much that he ordered the royal artist, Sir Godfrey Kneller, to paint Payne's portrait — which now hangs in the Cornish Museum in Truro.

Eventually, Payne retired to his native village of Stratton where he used his great strength to help the villagers when they needed him. Upon his death, locals found they could not get his oversized corpse down the twisting staircase from his upstairs bedroom, so they sawed through the floorboards and lowered his body by ropes onto the ground floor. Relays of strong pallbearers then carried that enormous coffin to Payne's grave-site near Stratton Church.

KING CHARLES II
"the never did a foolish thing, But never did a wise one."

CORNWALL – 16th.CENTURY

The Reformation, to begin with, did not make much difference to the religious life of the people or to the character of their church services.

"We will not receyve the new Service," they wrote, "because it is but lyke a Christmas game, but we wyll have our olde Service of Mattens, masse, evensong and procession, in Latten, as it was before. And we the Cornyshe men, whereof certain of us understand no Englyshe, utterly refuse thys newe Service." To this they further added, "We wyl have holy bread and holy water made every Sundaye; Palms and ashes at the tymes accustomed; Images to be set up again in every church, and all other auncient olde Ceremonyes used heretofore by our Mother the holy Church."

Up to this time every one in England was what we should now call a Roman Catholic, and the services were those of the Church of Rome.

The stained glass was in many cases taken out of the windows, rood screens were broken up, and the images and shrines of the saints destroyed. Nor were the people permitted any longer to worship in their old way. During the services, sidesmen paraded the church to see that none crossed themselves or used rosary beads when telling their prayers.

CORNWALL — 16th.CENTURY

*Memorial Plaque on Church Wall
— St. Ives*

ACCIDENTS IN THE MINES

Sudden death was a sad fact of life in the mining districts of Cornwall and was sometimes caused when a miner slipped as he climbed up and down the steep, perpendicular ladders that leant against the walls of deep mine shafts.

In the St. Mylor churchyard there is a tombstone that describes in amazing brevity how a miner died in this way:

> *HIS FOOT IT SLIP,*
> *AND HE DID FALL.*
> *HELP, HELP, HE CRIES*
> *AND THAT WAS ALL.*

There were many other causes of death in the Cornish mining industry because there were no work-safety rules in those bygone days and the rich mine-owners did not care, or even want to know, about the welfare of their workers.

To give the reader just one example of the frequency of mining tragedies, the Camborne Church Burial records state as many as nineteen deaths from mining accidents during just a part of the year 1835 — with the age of these miners ranging from 13 to 59.

Bennetts, Absolem, of Town (18) Injury received at Mine — 31 Mar.
Smith, Richard, of Town (21) From a hurt in a Mine — 2 April.
Jeffree, Henry, of Town (13) From a hurt in a Mine — 2 April.
Williams, John, of Puggis (27) Killed in a Mine — 15 May.
Chapple, John, of Cairn Entral (59) Hurt received in Mine — 24 July.
Littlejohn, James, of Penponds (21) Killed in a Mine — 22 Oct.
Bartle, Jilbert, of Town (35) Killed in a Mine — 22 Oct.

In 1863 nine men were killed at Botallack Mine when their skip (cage) crashed. Death was sharp and instantaneous because as the cage fell under the woodwork the huge beams decapitated them. All nine miners were fearfully injured in both head and body when the cage crashed downwards, like the rush of an avalanche, filling the shaft with thick clouds of dust and thousands of sparks of fire. Their bodies were recovered and buried in plain wooden coffins made in the carpenter's shop at the mine.

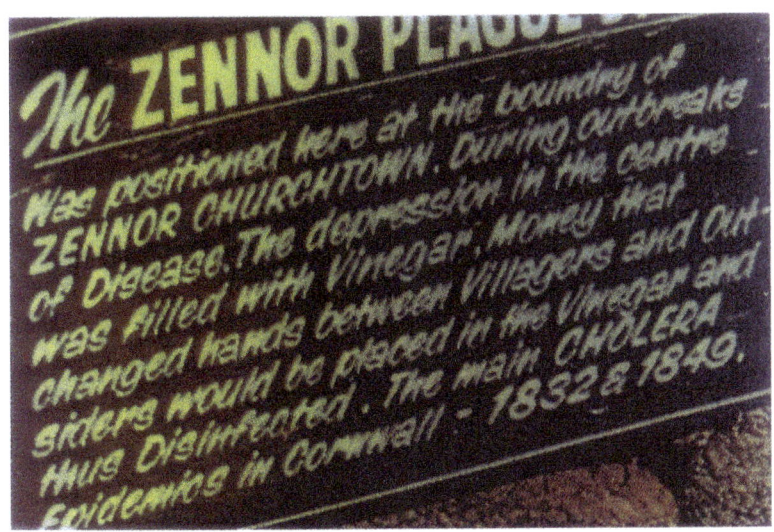

The Plague in Zennor
The Cholera Plaque reached England from Europe in October, 1831

Other tragedies recorded in that same year include an accident at the Carn Brea Mine where a man lost his leg during the blasting of a tunnel and consequently died from blood-poisoning.

Thirteen miners were killed at the Botallack Mine,

leaving several widows and almost forty children completely destitute.

At Penhall's Mine a man was killed by a descending kibble (an iron bucket) which struck him on the head as he was climbing up the ladder.

At Tolvadden Mine a young lad fell to his death between the 50 and 77 level; and at St. Just a miner slipped from the greasy rungs of a ladder to his death.

As for the Cornish women — many would be a widow by the age of 40, or sooner. She usually would be left with a large family to care for, yet knowing that all her sons would follow in their father's footsteps "into the mine" for that was their destiny. Is it any wonder that Cornwall became known as "The Land of Widows" until the mines closed down?

Restormel Castle — Ruins

A noonday rest for three weary farm-labourers who have been wielding their sickles since early morning to cut and bind wheat into sheaves. This scene is a typical one before the days of mechanical harvesters — they could move swiftly through the waving grain with great revolving arms, cutting and binding the sheaves as fast as thirty men.

TWO OLD HEADSTONES

Barely readable, this old headstone is leaning against the wall of the churchyard and belongs to WILLIAM SKEWES, late of the Parish of Gwinear, who departed this life on the 27th. December, (1807. Aged 73. (He was the son of William Skewes and he was baptized on the 21st. February, 1736.)

This is the grave of a miner in Stoke Climsland Churchyard. He was born in 1804, His death was caused by a careless action of his fellow miners and the story is written on this slate headstone.

TRURO

PADSTOW

Restormel Castle was built on the top of a high hill and looks down on the village of Lanlivery, in the Bodmin Parish. It dates back to the 13th Century and was once the palace of the Norman Earls of Cornwall. Abandoned for 400 years, it is now just a circular, ivy-covered ruin with a stone tower and deep moat.

Clockwise from top left: Truro Cathedral, Cheeswring Rocks, Lands End, Saltash Bridge (1859)

TWO OLD HEADSTONES

CAMBORNE PARISH CHURCH – granite, perpendicular style – restored in 1862

GUNNISLAKE – an old mining village in North Cornwall

BEDRUTHAN STEPS – rugged cliffs along the south coast

Cornwall's Rocky Coast

Cornish Tales

Dolly Pentreath, Mousehole fishwife and the last person to speak only Cornish.

St. Sampson's Holy Well

Celtic Cross

Phillack Churchyard (near Hayle) Cornwall.

Early Christian Monuments

Early Christian monuments in Cornwall were granite crosses — and there are still 350 remaining in the county. They can be found in churchyards (as above) or in fields and roadways. The tallest Celtic cross can be seen in Mylor — seventeen feet long it was used as a buttress against one of the church walls.

Slate headstone beside entrance to St. Gwinear Church.

HENRY HENDRA
Died 14th. July, 1819,
Aged 35 years.
HE WAS
An honest, sober and industrious
Miner
Whose Constant attendance within
These sacred walls
In the hours of public workship
Procured him the distinguishing
Epithet of
THE CHURCHMAN

In front of each church there was a LYCH GATE — a roofed gateway that leads into the church. Beneath the roof is the LYCH STONE on which the coffin bearers could rest the bier after carrying it, sometimes for many miles. They would have been exhausted, so there they sat to wait for the priest to lead them into the church.

SHEER CARELESSNESS

Although William Sampson was just another name in the parish records, his tombstone told me exactly how he had met his end. Here are the words inscribed upon his grave that lies close by the west wall of that little Cornish church: Stoke Climsland.

> *Sacred to the Memory of WILLIAM SAMPSON*
> *Of the Parish of Phillack in this County.*
> *He was killed in the Redmore Engine Shaft*
> *Thro' his comrades leaving a piece of Timber*
> *Slip thro' the lashing!*
> *April 7th. 1835. Aged 31 years.*
> *"Consider well, both young and old,*
> *Who by my grave do pass;*
> *Death soon may come with his keen scythe*
> *And cut you down like grass.*
> *Tho' some of you perhaps may think*
> *From danger to be free;*
> *Yet in a moment may be sent*
> *Into the grave like me."*

How then did my mining ancestor die? The tombstone says it all, although there is one more question I would like to ask. "Who paid for his expensive headstone?"

His widow certainly could not afford such a luxury. Obviously, his memorial was erected by those very same workmates who caused his death because it was the only way in which they could admit that he died through their carelessness.

It stands in Stoke Climsland as a permanent reminder to all the world that his mates were sorry. It must have been a financial burden upon them to pay for William's fine monument; but while other men lie in a churchyard unnoticed by passing travellers, at least his workmates made sure that William Sampson would never be forgotten.

THE DEATH OF JOHN MOYLE (1799-1857)

My great-grandmother, Hannah Moyle, had an older brother called John who was born in 1800 in the Parish of Wendron. He died while working down the mine.

Her brother's death is described by George Henwood in the 1858 book,

"Cornwall's Mining Journal". He describes the facts about Moyle's death after being a guest at that unfortunate man's funeral. Henwood writes:-

«We later found why so many miners were absent from work on that day. They had all come to bury John Moyle, we were told, and sure enough we found the village swarming with miners and their sweethearts, or wives; some had even travelled a distance of 14, or 15, miles to be there.

After a great deal of trouble we obtained a seat in the bar of the village inn which was crammed as full as it could possibly be. Here we met the landlord, a perfect specimen of a Cornish miner, who was in his element. He was surrounded by his fellowmen — and with a violincello in his hand he sang and played a great variety of hymns in admirable good taste.

For several hours the audience accompanied him "in frill chorus". I was not used to this unique Cornish custom of singing psalms and hymns in the taprooms of public houses, but these folks were in full swing. As "strangers" we were thus fully treated to what Wendron men could do.

In between the performance of various hymns, several men would take it in turn to step forward and describe the merits of the deceased miner.

As soon as the last hymn was finished, the landlord — an old Wendron miner — stepped forward and pressed me to drink a tot of rum, saying, "Take hold and drink, stranger, you are as welcome as we are!" Having complied, for it is an insult to refuse, I asked some questions of a youth who had been explaining the manner of the poor fellow's death to several other listeners:

"It was partly his own fault, sir; he was 58 years old and ought to have known better. I was in that part of the tunnel with him. Me and his son was working just above him, not more than 14 feet away. The old man was shovelling rubbish away from under the platform and his partner was breaking up the ore.

They had got a huge pile of ore broken up and ready to carry away on the platform. I dare say they must have had 5 tons upon that platform which is really too much — when his comrade struck the wall with his pick-axe and a great big stone moved. His comrade called out, "Stand out of the way, Uncle Jan, there's a big one coming — stand back, or you'll be killed!"

"Never mind," said the old man, "let her come." His son and me called out to the old man to stand out of the way, but instead of standing well back the old man moved right under the platform. He called out he was all right and safe under there.

As his comrade could not see him he thought the old man was out of the way, so he struck the big stone with his pick-axe again — and it came out of the wall and crashed onto the platform. The platform collapsed and down it came, rocks and all, upon the old man.

I heard him squeak and I jumped, God knows how, from where I was, over to him under the falling stones — I wonder I wasn't killed myself. We were beside him in two seconds, but he was all smashed up for he had the whole weight upon him.

We got him out from under the pile of rocks as soon as we could, but he was dead and a melancholy sight he was — but not half as *bad as his son who was to be pitied. He took on so — for 'tis bad to see a father killed in such a dreadful way."*

After this narration, one of Wesley's hymns was sung — the landlord leading with his violincello and giving out the words at the beginning of each verse. When this was finished, I enquired of the same miner as to the character of the deceased because seeing so many people present at his funeral I supposed he was something remarkable.

"He was a miner all his life, sir. His name was John Moyle and he used to work at West Basset Mine and many other large copper mines — he was a tributer (i.e. a miner who works at the mine face). He was a very steady man, sir, and saved up a good bit of his money instead of wasting it on drink.

He was a good-natured man and very much liked by everyone and almost everybody who knew him is here today and we are all sorry to lose 'im in such a wisht (terrible) way. If he had died in his bed we shouldn't have cared; but to be killed and smashed up like that seems hard; but I suppose that will be my end, too. We are all of us liable to end like that at any minute, and we know it.

I've seen many a young fellow killed down the mine, but not smashed up as bad as that. It was partly his own fault, yet his comrade blames himself for having too much ore on the platform. But he is now dead and gone and we hope his soul is gone to heaven."

After this we sang another hymn and then someone spoke again on the virtues of the deceased miner and his abilities down the mine; and not one person spoke of his vices. This is a wonderful trait of the Cornish character and it should put fashionable scandal to shame.

At 9 p.m. the inn was empty and the village deserted for everyone had to go a long way back to their homes.

CORNISH MINERS AT WORK

Miners have pale faces, indicating that the sun does not often shine upon them. They wear loose, woollen clothes, thick shoes without socks, and a strong hat with a convex crown (containing a hard lump of clay to protect the head from blows and stones).

THE WHEAL AGAR LIFT DISASTER

One of the worst disasters in Cornish mining history took place in the Wheal Agar copper mine during the 19th. Century. It happened on the 15th. August, 1883, when a cage containing a number of men was being drawn up to the surface.

The cage had almost reached its landing place at the top of the shaft when a wire rope snapped, causing the vehicle to hurtle back down the shaft — thus killing all twelve miners inside it.

Only one man, by sheer good luck, managed to spring out of the cage in the nick of time before it began its headlong descent to destruction.

The cage was made of iron and divided into two compartments, one above the other. It was so small that the miners travelling in the lower compartment could not stand, but sat on the floor. The cage had an opening on each side and a bar in the centre to which the men clung during its ascent, or descent.

An eyewitness described what happened in his own words:-

"*I was about to ring 'stop' as soon as I saw the heads of the miners in the upper compartment of the lift. But as the cage was slowly ascending I heard an unusual sound and glanced upwards to see what was happening. I perceived that the wire rope was parting from the wheel and then it suddenly snapped. Thomas Carbines was riding on top of the cage and he sprang off when he saw the broken rope swinging loosely in the air. The cage then rapidly disappeared from sight. I looked down into the shaft and heard the despairing cries of the men as their cage crashed against the wall. I was so frightened that I felt my blood almost turn to water."*

The cage was ripped apart as it struck the sides of the various levels. It hurtled downwards for hundreds of fathoms, turning over several times. A search party was immediately organised.

One body was found at the 110 level; two bodies were picked up at the 130; three were discovered at the 135; four at the 205; and two at the 225. In all cases the condition of the bodies was terrible.

According to a contemporary newspaper — *"Their brains were scattered all down the shaft and their death must have been as instantaneous as it was dreadful in its nature. Their bodies were smashed in an indescribable manner, their heads were reduced almost to a jelly as they were decapitated, and their limbs were torn off."*

The bodies — and pieces — were wrapped in rough flannel and made ready to be sent to the surface where their families and co-workers were waiting. As the cage had been destroyed, the bodies had to be brought up by ropes — and so hauled by hand to ground level.

An inquiry was conducted by a Government Inspector who later found that the wire rope used on this occasion was an old one and should never have been used for lifting men.

He also found that the cage had been grossly overloaded because only eight men should have been carried in it at any one time; yet ten persons were inside, with three more riding on top. This practice of riding on top of the cage was particularly dangerous.

However, the Inspector clearly attributed the Wheal Agar accident to the rotten condition of the wire rope, but added that such terrible consequences could have been avoided if only the cage had been fitted with safety catches. In the past, similar accidents had shown the need for safety catches to prevent cages falling in the event of ropes breaking.

Undoubtedly, the Wheal Agar disaster played its part in awakening opinion to the need to safeguard men's lives when they are using undergound winding equipment.

The thirteenth miner certainly had a remarkable escape when he jumped out of harm's way; but there are plenty more hairbreadth escapes from death recorded in the annals of Cornish mining.

HE GAVE HIS LIFE TO SAVE ANOTHER MAN

There were always brave men amongst the miners — men who were willing to help their workmates if they got into danger. For example, in September, 1863, an injured miner lay helplessly in an underground tunnel at Wentworth Mine, near Redruth, and he was about to be rescued by another miner, Joel Oats, who had volunteered to go down the deep shaft and bring up the injured man.

As Oats was being lowered down in the skip, the chain broke and that brave man was flung down the hole amidst an avalanche of dust and sparks of fire. Thus, he was dashed to pieces whilst attempting to rescue a suffering fellow creature and lost his life in a moment. Joel left a widow and seven small children, the eldest being only eleven years old—and the family was unprovided for.

A unique incident is recorded at St. Cleer stating that three deaths instead of one occurred. How could that be? Well, it seems that a miner named John Oliver was working in the South Caradon Mine, when he slipped and was caught in a flywheel that spun the poor man around so violently that not only were both his legs broken, but he also suffered serious internal injuries. He was carried home, but died as soon as he reached his own doorstep. He left a wife and eight children.

However, while the badly-injured body of John Oliver was being conveyed to his cottage, a young woman living nearby and thinking the stretcher contained her husband's dead body, screamed

hysterically and fell onto the ground in a deep faint. She then gave premature birth to a baby boy, but both died soon afterwards. So instead of one death, there were three.

TIN MINERS

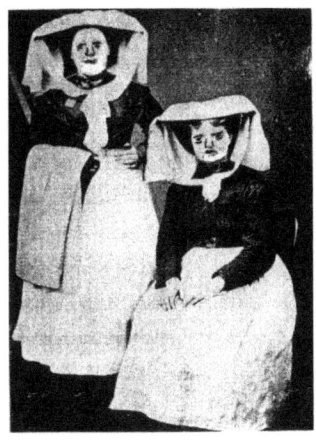

Miners waiting to go down Dolcoath Mine, Camborne. Circa 1900

The Cornish miners underground have pale countenances for the sun does not very often shine upon them. The miner is dressed in loose, woollen clothes and wears thick shoes without socks. On his head he wears a strong hat with a convex crown that contains a lump of clay which protects the miner's head from blows and falling stones.

BAL MAIDENS
These girls from Camborne, photographed at the end of the nineteenth century, were known as Bal Maidens. They worked at the mine surface, breaking up the larger pieces of copper ore and filling waggons. For this arduous work in 1880 they were paid only 14 pence a day. Until 1920 when fibre helmets and carbide lamps were introduced, the miners wore hats or 'tulls' made from compressed felt dipped in resin.

Captain Henry Skewes
1812 – 1881

A Mine Captain's uniform was a top hat and long coat with a velvet collar — to distinguish him from the ordinary miners working under his command.
(The Writer's great-grandfather)

Captain Henry Skewes 1812 — 1881

	CERTIFIED COPY of an ENTRY OF DEATH Pursuant to the Births and Deaths Registration Act 1953 HC 44							
	Death in the Sub-district of Phillack in the County of Cornwall							
	Registration District Penzance							
1	2	3	4	5	6	7	8	9
When and where died	Name and surname	Sex	Age	Occupation	Cause of death	Signature, description, and residence of informant	When registered	Signature of registrar
1852 Twelfth December Reawla Gwinear	Richard Martin Skewes	Male	18 years	Miner	Rheumatic Fever Certified	Henry Skewes Present at the death (father) Reawla Gwinear	Fifteenth December 1852	Thomas Bryant Registrar

My grandmother's seven brothers all worked down their local copper mine and this one died from rheumatic fever. It was not uncommon because miners worked in deep tunnels in temperatures up to 115 degrees with sweat running down their bodies — and then they had to walk home at the end of their shift in bitterly-cold wintry conditions.

83

A Cornish Miner

Statue of the 'LONE MINER' in Gunnislake

STAY IN THE PLACE WHERE YOU WERE BORN

The old Cornish folks were afraid to move away from the spot where they were born and in which they grew up. They became attached to their birthplace and very seldom left it, always retaining their old Celtic customs. Miners especially were superstitious and their creed was fatalistic. "I shall not die till my time comes," said the miner and fearlessly went to work down the mine.

But he firmly believed in signs, or omens, and if he met a woman on his way to the pit, he would return home and not go to work that day. Sadly, plenty of mining accidents occurred, — as in these two stories -

Hercules Jane, fourteen years old, died in a mining accident in September, 1859, and a witness at the inquest on this young lad's body was Thomas Moyle, a brother of my great-grandmother, Hannah Moyle, of Camborne. Thomas said, *"We were sinking a shaft (a deep hole) at Copper Hill Mine and about 8 p.m. we went up to the top level to sit down and have a smoke and the deceased lad, Hercules Jane, did the same.*

On returning to the top of the perpendicular ladder, we were about to climb down and I allowed Hercules to descend first When he was only a few feet away from us, the poor boy slipped from the greasy rungs and fell headlong down the shaft

Three fathoms down (about seven metres) we found him hanging, with one of his feet caught between the rungs of the ladder. We took him to the mine doctor and then carried him home, but he died from that fall a few hours later."

At Wheal Buller, a miner fell from the ladder when he paused to rest on the brace (a piece of wood that holds the ladder in place). Unfortunately, the rotten timber gave way and he fell and was killed.

The sketch above appeared in 1842, in Cyrus Redding's, "Illustrated Itinerary of Cornwall" and it was drawn at the time Rosetta Moyle was working at the Camborne mines. In fact, she could actually be one of the bal maidens featured in the foreground. The picture shows a typical mining scene with engine house, horse whim (left) and rope whim (right) for hauling the ore to the surface.

It was not unusual in those times to see very young children sent to earn a few pennies by breaking up the copper ore into smaller pieces and then separating them. Indeed, the Camborne census of 1841 gives many examples of child exploitation by the rich Mine Owners:-

James Eddy — a Miner, aged 7. Eliza Grundy — a Tin Dresser, aged 10. William Thomas — a Tin Miner, aged 13.

Of course, there was no free education in those days and a Miner's wage was so small that the whole family was forced to go out and find work. Both parents and children would issue forth from their humble cottage in the early morning and proceed to their labours in the local Mines_men below the surface and women and children above.

BOILER EXPLOSIONS

Once upon a time Cornwall was famous throughout the ancient world as "The Land of Tin", More than two thousand years before the birth of Jesus Christ this place was often visited by the Medes, Persians, Phoenicians and Greeks who came here to buy *'the white metal that does not rust'.*

Jews also came in their sailing ships to trade for the precious metal — and that is why smelting houses near Cornish tin mines were locally known as "Jews' Houses", There is an ancient legend which says Jesus visited Cornwall with his uncle, a wealthy merchant named Joseph of Arimathea.

But for the Cornishmen, seeking and digging for tin was a always a very dangerous occupation. They would spend ten hours of daylight in the darkness of a mine where the gloom was lit only by a candle stuck in a lump of clay upon their hard hats, Descending as much as three thousand feet into the bowels of the earth, a Cornish miner would toil in a labyrinth of black, steamy tunnels, risking his life daily — just for a few shillings a week.

Rock-falls, explosions, earth-subsidence, flooding, as well as cage and ladder accidents, have all been responsible for the deaths of workers in a tin mine.

The primitive, unprotected machinery used for crushing lumps of ore also caused many fatalities and injuries; yet, perhaps, the greatest danger of all was to be found in the boiler-houses of the pumping engines. Often these boilers were not adequately maintained by the engineers and consequently would frequently blow up with terrible consequences to any folks who happened to be in the vicinity.

Yet the boiler-house was a popular place for the miners who liked to dry their clothes in front of the great fire, but if an explosion occurred while men were in the building then casualties were obviously very high. Fortunately, the only sufferer in most of these boiler explosions was the engineman whose job it was to put coal on the fire and check the gauges.

The worst boiler explosion on record occurred at the United Hills Mine, near Porthtowan; and the engineman on duty at the time was James Sampson.

It was February, 1830, and winter had brought an intensely cold spell with snow and ice which is a rare sight in Cornwall whose climate is mild. The local ponds and pools were completely frozen over and many people were able to enjoy the unusual pleasure of skating on ice.

It was because of this bitterly-cold weather that as many as twelve people were in the boiler house on that particular day. About nine o'clock in the morning the boiler burst with such a tremendous explosion that people in the nearby cottages heard it and ran outside in fright.

Nine of the twelve people in that building were so dreadfully injured by the hot steam, scalding water and flying bricks that they died within a few hours in agonising pain. The other three folks survived, but were severely injured by horrific burns to their faces and hands.

On the following day an inquest was held at the mine and, according to the gruesome custom of the time, the nine bodies of those unfortunate victims were laid out on the floor for public viewing — although their burnt bodies were too terrible for most folks to want to look upon.

Jane Goyne gave evidence at the inquest. She was a balmaiden (tin-dresser) at the mine and had been very lucky to escape death. Jane described how she went with others into the boiler house on that bitterly-cold morning.

"It was just before nine o'clock," she said, "when I went with my sister, Elizabeth, into the boiler house to warm ourselves before work. The engineman, James Sampson, asked my sister to fetch him a jug of water. Elizabeth refused because she wanted to warm her hands by the fire, so I volunteered to get the water for Mr. Sampson."

"What happened next?" asked the Coroner.

"I had just left the boiler house," explained Jane, tearfully, "when I heard a tremendous explosion and looking back I saw a great column of steam rising up into the air. I was so scared that I ran home without looking back again."

"Where was your sister before the time of the explosion?" was the Coroner's next question.

"When I left, she was standing near the fireplace beside the others and the engineman was putting more coal on the fire."

"Can you identify your sister lying there?"

"Yes," replied Jane, bursting into tears as she pointed with a quivering finger at one of the bodies. "I can recognise pieces of the blue dress that she always wore to work, but there's not much left of her beautiful, long, black hair."

Mines played a big part in the lives of our Cornish ancestors for they all lived in areas where chimney stacks and mining buildings dominated the horizon for miles around and where the ground close to the mines was literally sown with miners' cottages. This was the dreary-looking world in which they lived and worked.

The mine owners boasted of untold riches stretching down into the bowels of the earth, but it was our mining ancestors who had to risk life and limb far below ground in a labyrinth of dark, steamy tunnels to obtain treasure for their masters.

The miner was very poorly-paid — and if he survived all the hazards of his job he died at an early age, anyway, from dust on his lungs (phthisis).

Like most Cornish boys, Henry Skewes worked in the mines from a young age. There was no compulsory, free education in those days so he probably would have started to dig for tin by the age of ten.

Cornwall's climate is a harsh one with plenty of rain, fog and gales. The days and nights are bitterly-cold for most months of the year and shelter from the cruel elements is not easily available. The young lad, Henry Skewis, would often go into the Engine House to keep warm.

One day Henry and two friends waited until most of the other workers had left the Engine House because they wanted some space to themselves in order to roast their potatoes over the fire.

However, just as they were about to go through the door carrying their basket of potatoes, an old woman hurried out of the Engine House and said to them, "My dear boys, don't go in there. I'm warning you. I think there is something wrong with the boiler."

The other two lads wanted to ignore the woman's warning and said to Henry, *"She's nothing but a stupid, old woman, so don't take any notice of what she said."*

They started to go inside, but Henry pulled them back from the door. "No, don't go inside. I think we should follow her advice — or we might be sorry."

So the three lads left that place and returned to the crushing-house where they were loading ore into the waggons.

Only a few minutes later the boiler burst — killing the engineman and the only other person that was in there, a woman named Ruby Lugg.

The three boys fell down on their knees, thanking God that they had escaped such a sudden, hideous death; and there and then on bended knee they made a sacred promise to devote the rest of their lives to God's service.

And so they did. They eventually became lay-preachers and Sunday School teachers in the Camborne Wesleyan Society.

Explosion in the Mine

FACT OR FICTION

"And did those feet in ancient times
Walk upon England's mountains green?
And was the Holy Lamb of God
On England's pleasant pastures seen?"
And did the countenance divine
Shine forth upon our clouded hills?"

The great hymn writer, William Blake, in the above lines from his well-known hymn *Jerusalem* is referring to that ancient tradition which claims that Jesus visited Britain, first as a boy and later as a young man.

It has always been a strong legend in Cornwall and believed by the old folks, that Jesus came to their county in particular — and perhaps this claim is not as impossible as it may sound.

After all, who can really tell us what happened to Jesus during those "hidden years" and I refer to the twenty years of His life that are unaccounted for in the four Gospels.

Jewish authorities seem to agree that Mary became a widow when Jesus was still young; indeed, at the last mention of Joseph as still alive in the Gospels, Jesus was only 12 years old (Luke ch. 2, v. 43)

It is generally thought that until he was thirty Jesus stayed at home in Nazareth carrying on Joseph's work as the village-carpenter in order to support his widowed mother — there is no actual, written proof in the Gospels to support this claim, is there?

According to the Talmud (a book of Jewish Law) Joseph of Arimathaea was an uncle of the Virgin Mary and therefore Jesus's great-uncle. In those days, the guardianship of a fatherless son was the responsibility of an uncle and so this responsibility for Jesus may indeed have rested upon the shoulders of Joseph of Arimathaea.

In the New Testament we are told that Joseph was a member of the Jewish Sanhedrin (Great Council) and that on the evening of the Crucifixion he *'begged the body of Jesus'* from Pontius Pilate and buried it in his own rock-hewn tomb (Luke ch. 23, v. 50-53).

As Jesus's great-uncle his action therefore agrees with both Roman and Jewish law that states the nearest relative should dispose of a dead man, no matter how he died.

The Greek texts of Mark and Luke describe Joseph as an *'honourable counsellor'* and in the Latin Vulgate a reference is made to him as *'Decurio'*; whilst in the book of Jerome he is given the title *'Nobilis Decurio'* meaning that Joseph was an officer in charge of metal mines, or he may even have been the *'Minister of Mines'* for the Romans.

It is therefore obvious that Joseph would know all about the tin and lead mines in Cornwall and probably took his merchant ships there to purchase the tin ingots and carry them back to Mediterranean countries.

In olden times, Cornish tin miners would chant as they worked, *"Joseph was a tin man"*; also, an old Cornish Christmas carol praises Joseph, describing him as *"a tinner who sailed the seas"*

Even Julius Caesar wrote about the tin-industry in Cornwall after he landed with his cohorts in Britain in 55 B.C. and uttered those famous words, *"Veni, vidi, vici"* ("I came, I saw, I conquered").

If we study Jesus' ministry we can see that He knew about the world and the problems of life for His teachings reveal the knowledge of a travelled man — after all most men who travelled in those days were sailors — so Jesus could have been with His uncle, perhaps on Joseph's ship as its carpenter.

If Jesus was not at home in Nazareth during those twenty years of His life that are unaccounted for in the Gospels, then it is very likely He was working and travelling with His great-uncle. And why not to Cornwall where tin was mined, smelted into ingots and exported to the then known world? Legends should not be dismissed as pure fiction.

(This article is based on a book by Glyn Lewis, entitled, "And Did Those Feet?")

And Jesus opened his mouth, and taught them, saying, "Blessed are the poor in spirit; for theirs is the kingdom of heaven. Blessed are they that mourn; for they shall be comforted. Blessed are the meek; for they shall inherit the earth. Blessed are they which do hunger and thirst after righteousness; for they shall be filled. Blessed are the merciful; for they shall obtain mercy. Blessed are the pure in heart; for they shall see God. Blessed are the peacemakers; for they shall be called the children of God. Blessed are they which are persecuted for righteousness' sake; for theirs is the kingdom of heaven. Blessed are ye when men shall revile you, and persecute you, and shall say all manner of evil against you falsely, for my sake. Rejoice, and be exceeding glad; for so persecuted they the prophets that were before you."

INFANT TRAGEDIES

Many years ago, a poor woman residing in the little mining village of St. Gwinear experienced a most distressing ordeal. In those far-off days, miners' wives had to feed large families on the miserable pittance their husbands earned down the local copper mines. Their houses were very humble and had 'stable-doors' that opened directly onto the rough and stony main street. It was during the year 1860, on a hot summer's day, when this hard-working woman placed her baby in a cradle on the floor before going to the local well to fetch a pail of water.

In her haste to carry out this tedious chore, the poor woman forgot to close the bottom half of the 'stable-door'. Now in those days Cornish folks let their pigs and chickens live in the street because they could forage for food in the hedgerows, or wander across the grassy areas of common land.

After a short interval the woman returned and noticed the bottom part of the front door was wide open. To her horror on entering the room she saw a huge pig standing near her baby and when she looked into the cradle the child's clothes were covered with blood and both hands were missing.

The screams of that unfortunate woman brought all the villagers running to her door to see what was wrong. The poor little fellow was still alive and with care finally recovered, except for the loss of his hands. *"Never mind,"* they said, *"he can earn money as a freak at the country fairs."*

The following fatal accident occurred in a Cornish village near the beginning of the 19th. Century. A tiny infant experienced the worst fate that one could possibly imagine when his mother left the house to fetch her two older children from the nearby grandmother's dwelling.

Before departing, this mother placed her tiny infant upon the bed, closing the door carefully behind her. Unknowingly, the woman shut a young pig inside the house with the baby — this animal had wandered in from the street while she was busy in the kitchen at the back of the house and so she did not notice it.

After a short interval the mother returned to the house with her older children and began busily cooking the evening meal, supposing the baby to be fast asleep. Some minutes later, to her utter astonishment and horror, as she happened to be passing the bed she witnessed a terrible scene. Somehow, that stray pig which she had accidentally shut up inside the house, had climbed upon the bed and was then in the very act of devouring the child.

The mother's shrieks brought the neighbours to her side, but they were too late to prevent the calamity — and also too late to render assistance to the baby. The child's face had been torn to pieces and devoured — and the hands and feet of the ill-fated, innocent babe were also mangled and destroyed.

An Inquest held on the same day acquitted the distraught parent of any blame whatsoever. The ferocious pig was shot immediately after the accident was discovered. It was then burnt by order of the Coroner — for obvious reasons.

TO CORNISH LADS WHO FELL IN THE GREAT WAR

Germany started war with the cry, "World domination, or downfall!" so our brave lads quickly sprang to arms and joined the Duke of Cornwall's Regiment. Together, even while fierce gales blew in from the Channel and fog filled the valleys, they arose as one, both rich and poor, leaving tiny granite cottages or fine country mansions, to defend Cornwall, our Empire and the world. Through God's goodness they and their allies won victory in 1918, yet at a mighty sacrifice of life — and a glorious part of that sacrifice was given by these Cornish lads whose graves now lie far off in foreign fields.

ENGLAND"S MOST FAMOUS SAILOR

This story is about Sir Francis Drake who was born in the village of Tavistock (which is on the Cornwall/Devon border). There were twelve boys in his family, yet Francis was the only one who expressed a desire to go to sea, so his father apprenticed him to the master of a small ship in Plymouth harbour. Thus began Drake's career at sea which eventually led to his daring adventures in the West Indies and the Spanish Main.

Drake is best known for his brilliant seamanship and audacious courage which enabled him to destroy the mighty Spanish Armada when it sailed up the English Channel on its way to conquer England in 1588. The reader has surely heard how Drake was playing his favourite game of bowls on Plymouth Hoe with his officers at the time.

When news was brought that the enemy had been sighted off the Lizard, Howard was eager to stop the game and put to sea immediately, but Drake insisted on finishing the game saying, *"There's plenty of time to win this same and thrash the Spaniards too"*.

Drake also enjoyed another game which he called, *'Singeing the King of Spain's beard'*. This sport involved sailing into Cadiz harbour under cover of darkness and by using 'fireships' he would burn as many Spanish vessels as he could before escaping back to Plymouth. No wonder Drake's actions inspired terror in the hearts of England's enemy.

For several years Sir Francis Drake was Lord Mayor of Plymouth and did many good works for that city. He had channels dug and the construction of a reservoir to bring fresh clean water to the people from nearby Dartmoor — and he had a flour-mill constructed to make fresh bread for the Plymouth residents.

Sir Francis Drake married the daughter of a poor Cornish fisherman. Perhaps he saw this pretty young maiden as she helped her father upon the shores of the River Tamar at a place called Saltash — which is on the Cornish side of the river. But did she die soon after their marriage? Nothing is mentioned about her in history books, or in the Plymouth museum where Drake's personal belongings are stored. However, Mary's simple grave is in the churchyard at Higher St. Budeaux — which the writer saw many years ago — and the humble cottage where she lived in Saltash (Cornwall) has been preserved and can be visited by tourists.

Sir Francis Drake married Mary Newman, daughter of a poor Cornish fisherman.

Sir Francis Drake was already famous as the first Englishman to sail a ship around the world, and for his daring attacks on Spanish treasure ships, when the Spanish King Philipe II, decided to launch an invasion of England. In 1588 the Spanish Armada set sail with over 130 ships including 2,000 cannon. The smaller and outgunned English fleet waited in Plymouth harbour as the vast Spanish fleet sailed by. Drake

Sir Francis Drake c1543-1596

had time to finish a famous game of bowls on the Hoe while the fleet passed him in full view. Only when the Armada had moved to the east of Plymouth did the English fleet set sail, taking advantage of the south-westerly winds to make attacks on the enemy. The Spanish anchored at Calais awaiting reinforcements from Holland. This is when Drake and his ships took advantage of the situation. On the night of 7th August they sent fire ships into the Spanish position. This caused so much confusion in the dark that the fleet scattered leaving the flag-ship at the mercy of the English fleet. Harried all the way round the Scottish coast the enemy finally returned to Spain having lost half of the greatest sailing fleet ever assembled.

DANGER FROM FIRE

The average wage of a tin miner in the 1860's was about 2 shillings a week, so it is amazing how their wives managed to bring up large families, feed and clothe them, pay the rent, and keep the fire burning on such a miserable pittance.

Therefore, it is not surprising that from necessity even the smallest children were expected to do jobs — often far beyond their capabilities — in order to earn a few pennies for food.

It does seem strange nowadays to think of two little boys, aged seven and four, being left all day on their own in a farmer's field to scare away a flock of thieving crows.

On the 1st. April, 1839, two young boys were told to stay in the cornfield all day to guard the farmer's valuable crop. Later, seven-year old Thomas would describe, as best he could, what happened on that fateful day to his little brother.

My brother, John, who is only four years old, went with me into the field to shoo away the crows. Frederick, my older brother, built a fire in the middle of the Held for us to sit beside and warm ourselves.

Frederick brought a tinder-box into the field from father's house by which he got a light to start the fire burning — and we had to gather sticks from the hedge to keep it alight all day as we needed to keep ourselves warm for it was a bitterly-cold wind.

About 4 o'clock that afternoon my young brother was close to the fire and he was breaking up sticks to put on the fire. His back was turned away from the fire and he was bending over, using his foot to break up the thin branches.

Suddenly he lost his balance and fell backwards into the flames. I heard him shout, "Help!" so I turned around and saw him trying to pull himself out by the tufts of grass, but by that time all his clothes were ablaze.

He was wearing a long, cotton pinafore and a big cotton handkerchief around his neck. I ran to him and tried to put out the flames, but could not.

John was screaming and Willy Rodda who was working in a nearby field, ran and put out the flames, but my poor brother died immediately from the terrible burns all over his body.

FROM CROW-SCARING TO WESTMINSTER

The story of George Edwards is entitled *"From Crow-Scaring to Westminster"* because he became a British politician in spite of his humble beginnings. Edwards was born into a very poor Cornish family and personally experienced the curse of poverty. He knew what it was like to see his mother with an empty purse and therefore he went out to work for a neighbouring farmer, scaring away the crows in return for a bit of food.

Edwards grew up to become a farm-labourer and later fought for the formation of a workers' union to improve working conditions and wages. He was elected as their leader in the 1880's and the following folk-song was written in praise of his great work that brought about the National Union of Agricultural Workers.

An Old Cornish Cottage
A Farewell to George Edwards
(Sung to the tune "My grandfather's Clock)

My grandfather said in the noontide of life,
    Poverty was a grief and a curse;
For it brought to his home sorrow, discord and strife,
    And kept him poor, with empty purse.
So he took a bold stand and joined the union band,
    To help his fellow men he tried;
    A union man he vowed he'd stand
    Till the day he died.
My grandfather's dead; as we gathered round his bed,
    These last words to us he did say:
'Don't let your union drop nor the agitation stop,
    Or else you will soon rue the day.
Get united to a man for it's your only plan,
    Make the union your care and your pride.
    Help on reform in every way you can.'
    Then the old man died.

HELSTON"S ANCIENT CUSTOMS

Cornwall's most famous folk-song is the Helston Furry Dance Song (sometimes known as the 'Cornish May Song'). The tune is a catchy one and by some strange quirk of fortune it achieved 'top of the pops' status in Britain during 1978. The word "Furry" is from the Celtic word 'Feur' (meaning 'Holiday' or 'Fair').

It does not seem folk-songs (whatever country they may belong to) will ever go completely out of fashion because they have already stood the true test of time. They are the golden oldies of yesteryear and will still be sung after much of our modem rubbish has been forgotten. Folk-songs have good strong lyrics and memorable tunes.

In ancient Cornwall as soon as the month of May arrived it was the custom to gather hawthorn blossom from the hedgerows to decorate the cottages and gardens. Working-class folks would celebrate the beginning of Summer in this ancient, time-honoured, Celtic ritual. Young folks would rise early and go into the woods to gather branches of

Dancing Round the Maypole

greenery and hawthorn blossom with which to brighten up their homes after the long, dark, dreary days of winter. Then the villagers would erect a tall wooden Maypole, decorated with ribbons and flowers, upon the village green to be the centre of merrymaking.

However, during the Commonwealth period of English history, stern-faced Puritans (especially Oliver Cromwell) regarded the Maypole as a 'stinking idol' and complained that barely one third of young girls who visited the woods on the eve of May Day returned undefiled.

As one wit wrote back in the 17th. Century; *"Hooray! Hooray! The First of May! Outdoor sex begins today!"* Sadly, the 20th. Century saw the demise of many old Cornish traditions because of the tragedy of two world wars and, later, the increase in annual paid-holidays for workers; but especially because of modern inventions that brought about more popular forms of mass entertainment — cinema, radio and television.

However, there are still two places in Cornwall that celebrate the first day of the Celtic Summer with even more passion than in olden times — mainly to attract the tourist-dollars, perhaps! I refer to Padstow (a fishing village in the north of Cornwall) and to Helston (a rural town in Cornwall's far west). Both places have their own unique folk-song and festivities, but I think Helston's annual celebrations are probably better known.

Helston's folk-song was first officially printed in 1802, accompanied by historical notes about that quaint old Cornish town — which I quote beneath: -

"The inhabitants of Cornwall, being a remnant of the Ancient Britons, still retain some of their ancient customs (as do the Welsh and the Scots) This old traditional ballad is the source of great merrymaking to the inhabitants of the town and neighbourhood of Helston where it is always sung and danced by them on the eighth of May when they welcome in the summer with peculiar and unique

A Worker

forms of rejoicing, revelry, festivity and mirth. Their custom is this — at the break of day the common people of the town arise early and go into the fields and woods to gather all kinds of flowers to decorate their hats and bosoms; to enjoy the flowery meadows and listen to the chirping of the birds. If during their wanderings they find a person at work he is severely punished. They make him their prisoner and carry him on a pole to the nearest river across which he must leap, or else fall in, but leap he must or pay money to them. After this simple sport is ended, they then return to the town bearing green hawthorn and sycamore boughs which represent the coming of summer to their homes. They then form themselves into various dancing groups of lads and lasses and they jig it all over the town; claiming a right to dance through any person's house. They go in one door and out the other and through the garden; and thus in and out the houses they dance happily and so right through the town from one end to the other — thus they continue until it is dark."

The original words to this Helston folk-song are not at all like the modern ones as the ancient version praises St. George (the patron saint of England) and Robin Hood (England's romantic outlaw).

> *Saint George next shall be our song, Saint George he was a knight, O;*
> *Of all the kings in Christendom King Geòrgie is the right, O.*
> *In every land that e'er we gô, sing halan tow and George, O,*
> *Sing halan tow and Georgie, O.*

THE HELSTON FLORAL DANCE

As I walked home on a summer night when stars in heaven were shining bright;

Far away from the footlight's glare, into the sweet and scented air of a quaint old Cornish town.

Born from afar on a gentle breeze, joining the murmur of summer seas, Distant sounds of an old world dance, played by the village band per chance, on the calm air came a-floating down.

I thought I could hear the curious tone of the cornet, clarinet and big trombone; fiddle, cello, big base drum, bassoon, flute and euphonium.

Far away as in a trance, I heard the sound of the floral dance.

And soon I heard such a bustling and prancing, and then I saw all the villagers dancing;

In and out of the houses they came, old folk, young folk, all the same,

In that quaint old Cornish town.

Every boy had a girl by the waist, and carried her on with abandoned haste, whether they knew one another I cared not, whether they cared at all I know not, but they kissed as they danced along.

And there was the band with the curious tone of the cornet, clarinet and big trombone; fiddle, cello, big base drum, bassoon, flute and euphonium. Each one making the most of his chance altogether in the Floral dance.

I felt so lonely standing there and I could only stand and stare, for I had no maid with me, lonely I should have to be in that quaint old Cornish town. When suddenly hastening down the lane, a figure I knew I saw quite plain. With outstretched hands I dashed along and carried her into that merry throng, and fiddle and all went dancing on.

We danced around to the curious tone of the cornet, clarinet and big trombone, fiddle, cello, big base drum, bassoon, flute and euphonium.

Each one making the most of his chance, altogether in the floral dance.

Dancing here and dancing there,
Even dancing everywhere.
Up and down and round about —
HURRAH FOR THE CORNISH FLORAL DANCE!

AT A CORNISH FAIR

All through the Middle Ages and later, May Day was a public holiday. And everywhere in England it was observed with all kinds of frolicking. At dawn, everyone went to gather flowers and evergreen boughs and in the middle of the village green a Maypole was set up for maidens to dance around, winding its long ribbons in and out. The prettiest maid was chosen to be the May Queen.

The sun is a-shining to welcome the day
With a heigh-ho come to the fair!
The folk are all singing so merry and gay,
Heigh-ho come to the fair.
All the stalls on the green are as fine as can be,
With trinkets and tokens so pretty to see,
So it's come then maidens and men
To the fair in the pride of the morning.

*So it's come then maidens and men
To the fair in the pride of the morning.
So lock up your house, there'll be plenty of fun,
And it's heigh-ho come to the fair!
For love-making too, if so be you've a mind
Heigh-ho come to the fair!
For hearts that are happy are loving and kind,
Heigh-ho come to the fair!*

"You must wake and call me early, call me early, mother dear;
For I'm to be Queen of the May, mother, I'm to be Queen of the May."

COCK-FIGHTING

*Cock-Fighting–a popular
entertainment in Cornwall
Long spikes attached to the cocks' legs
made the fighting cruel and savage*

In 1849 an act passed by the British Parliament brought an end to the cruel sport of cock-fighting. There was a severe penalty of 5 pounds for each day a person continued to break the law by keeping and training fighting-cocks.

It was a common sport among both Greeks and Romans

in ancient times and later flourished in England for six centuries and was even patronised by royalty. In the mining villages of Cornwall it was a popular sport, both for pleasure and profit.

Today, although this brutal and barbaric blood sport is considered illegal in Western countries, cock-fighting is still a tradition in Asian places such as Bali, India and Timor. In villages where this cruel sport is still carried on, fighting-cocks in cages can be seen outside humble-looking houses.

No doubt much skill is required in the training of cocks, especially in preparing the cock for combat by fastening onto its legs the steel spurs with which it can tear an opponent to pieces. The experienced fighting-cock can be a very dangerous bird — a desperate killer because in the ring it knows it must fight for its very survival.

Two specially-bred birds known as gamecocks are placed in a ring to fight. The roosters are specially trained to severely injure and kill one another and are even tormented by the owner to make them more aggressive in the ring. During a fight the birds peck and maim one another with their beaks and tear flesh with their fitted steel spurs-and the fight only ends when one of them is dead, or too weak to fight. The loser gets thrown onto the rubbish heap, sometimes while still alive.

In the year 1824 a fighting-cock escaped from its cage one summer's day and strutted down the main street of Ludgvan, a mining village in West Cornwall. Suddenly it noticed a group of young children happily playing on the grass outside a tiny cottage and for some unexplained reason this escaped gamecock decided to attack them.

Choosing the smallest child, no more than a toddler, the fighting-cock charged into the little group, running fast forward with neck and wings outstretched and its head lowered. The sharp beak was wide open as the bird made a continuous hissing sound. Its scraping claws raised a thick cloud of dust which momentarily hid the child and her attacker.

The other small children watched helplessly, too terrified to even run away. From inside the nearest cottage, a woman heard their screams and rushed outside to find the cause of all the commotion. The cock repeatedly poked the toddler's face with its pointed beak, at the same time ripping the child's chest with its long claws. Then it knocked its victim onto the ground.

Before the woman could find a stout stick to use as a weapon, the cock had repeated its vicious attacks upon the child until blood was oozing through her thin cotton pinafore and pouring down the little body. By the time the woman got there to beat the cock off, the child was covered with blood and crying piteously. Blood was running freely from the child's eyes, nose, mouth and head; the poor toddler was so ill after receiving such terrible wounds that she died the next day. As for that ferocious rooster, it continued its career in the world of cock-fighting.

BULL-BAITING

The conduct of ordinary people during those early centuries in Cornwall was often much worse than one cares to imagine. Even up to the beginning of the nineteenth century cruel sports such as cock-fighting, bull-baiting, bear-baiting and badger-baiting were quite common and popular.

The remains of old cock pits may still be found today in remote parts of Cornwall. They were cruel places where game-cocks had little steel spurs fastened to their legs and beaks sharpened to make them more deadly in a duel to the death with another bird.

Yet bull-baiting was an even more brutal and degrading pastime amongst the working classes and this cruel sport was popular, particularly in West Cornwall.

Imagine a dull, wintry day as an old bull is being led through the streets of Penzance. The animal has been adorned with colourful ribbons to add a touch of revelry to the occasion and surrounding this unfortunate animal we see a savage-looking crew of noisy men and boys, eager to feast their eyes upon the bull's torture and suffering.

After dragging the wretched beast through several crowded streets, the leader of the gang announces to the assembled company that a fight to the death will take place on the following day.

At ten o'clock the next morning this poor bull is led out into the field of torture where, like a lamb to the slaughter, it allows itself to be fastened to a stake placed in the middle of the arena. Then burning pepper is blown into its nostrils to make it more furious; and then rowdy onlookers place bets with promotors on the outcome of the fight.

After the bets have been placed, four big dogs are let loose to worry and bite this wretched animal; and whilst two dogs attract the bull's attention with a direct frontal attack, the other two bite and tear at its fleshy sides and hind legs.

Perhaps you can now see why the bulldog of our present day derives its name from this cruel, barbaric sport? Because its nose, being well set-back between the eyes, allows the dog to breathe when its teeth are fastened into the flesh of the bull.

Without any rest, this unfortunate bull is continually worried and bitten by the dogs for almost five hours until it collapses, exhausted and in terrible pain, onto the ground. It will be a considerable time before it can struggle to its legs again.

But while the exhausted bull is lying on the ground, those ferocious dogs are encouraged to gnaw and tear away at its flesh, though keeping well out of range of the bull's sharp horns.

However, in spite of the mangled and bloody state of the animal, its brutal tormentors are proposing to continue the fight in a week's time. They intend to find a farmer who will put it to grass for a few days in order that they might have more sport out of it.

The chief reason to use the same bull for another fight is that the savage dogs on this occasion have not actually pinned its head to the ground and torn out its tongue; for unless the tongue is cleanly pulled out of the animal's face there is no final decision as to the winner and therefore bets cannot be honoured.

Happily for the poor beast, its torturers could not find someone willing to feed it for a week because grass is rather scarce in winter — the date being 17th. December, in the year 1817.

Perhaps this unfortunate bull died from its wounds before it could be tormented any further. Let us hope so.

BADGER-BAITING

Even as late as the year 1857, the cruel sport of badger-baiting was still being enjoyed by the lower classes. It was certainly a favourite pastime amongst poor miners in the Redruth and Camborne districts.

A badger is a very heavy beast, often weighing as much as 40 pounds and usually its owner would issue a challenge by boasting that his animal was willing to fight anybody's dog for a wager.

BROCK the BADGER

At one time in Cornwall badgers were even a part of the poor man's diet and greatly esteemed, especially when the hindquarters were cured as ham. Badgers are still eaten with relish in China.

The badger is a sturdily-built mammal with short legs and powerful jaws. Its body is covered with long, coarse,

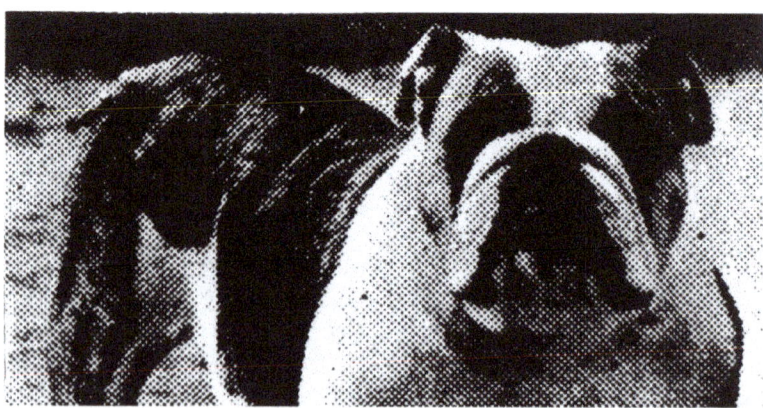

black hair and usually it is an inoffensive creature, but when attacked, the badger will put up a courageous defence.

Eventually, badger-baiting was prohibited by the middle of the nineteenth century, but was illegally continued in Cornwall for several more years.

Fortunately, the teaching of John Wesley had its greatest effect upon the Cornish by the middle of the nineteenth century; and so, together with the weight of the Law, religion put an end to Cornwall's rampant evils of drunkenness, smuggling, wrecking and brutal sports such as bull-baiting, badger-baiting and cock-fighting.

Richard Martin, a Member of Parliament, was the man most responsible for introducing bills to prevent cruelty to animals. Hence his nickname 'Humanity Martin'. In 1822 his Bill became law and for the first time in England — indeed, for the first time in any country in the world — a law protected animals against the cruelty of man. Martin spent many years taking action against offenders, taking them to court to be fined.

At the Westminster Pit one could see Jacco, the fighting monkey, matched against vicious dogs. At Clerkenwell, one could see 'a mad ball dressed up with fireworks, turned loose, with a cat tied to the bull's tail. Likewise, a dog dressed up with fireworks and turned loose'.

Not until 1835 was bull-baiting made illegal in England. Other sports which showed British brutality to animals were cock-fighting, dog-fighting, bear-baiting and cock-throwing (i.e. tying a fowl to a post and throwing sticks at it).

Facts of 1500"s in Cornwall

Most people got married in June, because they took their yearly bath in May, and they still smelled pretty good by June.

However, since they were starting to smell, brides carried a bouquet of flowers to hide the body odour.

Hence the custom today of carrying a bouquet when getting married

Baths consisted of a big tub filled with hot water. The man of the house had the privilege of the clean water, then all the other sons and men, then the women and finally the children.

Last of all the babies. By then the water was so dirty you could actually lose someone in it.

Hence the saying, "Don't throw the baby out with the bath water".

Houses had thatched roofs, with thick straw piled high and no wood underneath. It was the only place for animals to be warm, so all the cats and other small animals (mice, bugs) lived in the roof.

When it rained it became slippery and sometimes the animals would slip and fall off the roof.

Hence the saying, "It's raining cats and dogs."

There was nothing to stop things from falling into the house. This posed a real problem in the bedroom, where bugs and other droppings could mess up your nice clean bed.

Hence a bed with big posts and a sheet hung over the top offered some protection — and canopied beds came into existence.

ST. IVES HARBOUR

The floor was dirt. Only the wealthy had something other. Hence the saying, "Dirt poor".

The wealthy had slate floors that would get slippery in the winter when wet, so they spread thresh (straw) on the floors to keep their footing.

As the winter wore on, they added more thresh until, when you opened the door, it would all start slipping outside, so a piece of wood was placed in the entranceway. Hence, a thresh hold.

In those old days, they cooked in the kitchen with a big kettle that always hung over the fire. Every day they lit the fire and added things to the pot.

They ate mostly vegetables, and did not get much meat. They would eat the stew for dinner, leaving leftovers in the pot to get cold overnight, and then start over the next day.

Sometimes stew had food in it that had been there for quite a while.

Hence the rhyme: "Peas porridge hot, peas porridge cold, peas porridge in the pot nine days old."

Sometimes they could obtain pork, which made them feel quite special. When visitors came, they would hang up their

HAYLE HARBOUR

bacon to show off. It was a sign of wealth that a man could "bring home the bacon".

They would cut off a little to share with guests and would all sit around and chew the fat.

Those with money had plates made of pewter. Food with high acid content caused some of the lead to leach on to the food, causing lead poisoning deaths. This happened most often with tomatoes, so for the next 400 years or so, tomatoes were considered poisonous.

Bread was divided according to status. Workers got the burnt bottom of the loaf, the family got the middle, and guests got the top, or the upper crust.

Lead cups were used to drink ale or whisky. The combination would sometimes knock the imbibers out for a couple of days. Someone walking along the road would take them for dead and prepare them for burial.

They were laid out on the kitchen table for a couple of days and the family would gather around and eat and wait to see if they would wake up.

Hence the custom of "holding a wake".

England is old and small and the local folks began to run out of places to bury people, so they would dig up coffins and take the bones to a bone-house, and reuse the grave.

When reopening these coffins, one of 25 coffins were found to have scratch marks on the inside, and they realized they had been burying people alive.

So they would tie a string on the wrist of the corpse, lead it through the coffin and up through the ground and tie it to a bell.

Someone had the duty of sitting out in the graveyard all night (the graveyard shift) to listen for the bell; thus someone could be "saved by the bell" or was considered "a dead ringer".

And that's the truth. Who said history was boring!

THE STAG

Before the invention of the internal combustion engine, villagers had to walk everywhere. If folks did not, or could not, walk they would be confined to just visiting relatives and friends within their own village.

However, if a long journey was absolutely necessary then people would take the shortest route possible — usually across a roadway-field to avoid the much longer way around.

By crossing a stile (a series of wide, stone steps through a narrow gap in the hedge) a walker could thus shorten his journey. In fact, stiles were plentiful in every part of Cornwall, but apparently in the parish of Zennor there were no fewer than seventy of them.

These wide, deep gaps between flat stones allowed folks to enter the field, yet prevented animals from escaping. According to the common laws of England, farmers were not allowed to keep a dangerous animal in a roadway field as people had the right-of-way.

It was the year 1866 — and although a public footpath ran through a field leading to Porthmear village, the farmer broke the law by keeping a large stag in it. The local villagers knew about this dangerous animal and were so afraid of it that they preferred to take the long way around across Ulford Bridge to Porthmear, rather than walk past that fierce red buck.

Young Richard Tremellan had been warned to keep away from the stag that lived in the roadway-field leading to his grandmother's cottage, but he ignored his mother's words because it was a hot day and he felt tired.

It was Springtime and the buck was restless. Completely

oblivious to any danger, Richard decided to step over the stile and walk across the roadway field.

His mother had baked some delicious pasties that morning and wanted him to take one to grandmother as a special treat for her dinner. He carried it, wrapped carefully in a linen cloth to keep it hot.

Perhaps the young lad was hungry and wanted to return home as quickly as possible to eat his own pasty. There must have been some good reason for Richard's decision to cross that roadway-field, but did he really think the great red buck would not see him?

Inevitably, the stag caught the scent of a stranger in the wind and lifted its great head. If Richard had only retreated the short distance he had already come he would have been

safe, but instead he thought he could outrun the stag to the end of the path.

The huge animal, however, had other ideas and would not allow the boy to cross unmolested. It stopped grazing and lowering its great antlers in a menacing way began moving slowly towards him. Richard, not realising his immediate danger, stopped and turned around to confront the animal.

At that very moment the stag gave a mighty roar and advanced more quickly, still shaking its antlers and rolling its eyes in anger at this daring invader of his territory.

Field labourers at work in an adjoining field were aroused from their job of planting potatoes at the sound of the stag's bellowing. Only then did they notice the boy and the danger he was facing, but before they could run to his aid they witnessed the inevitable outcome.

In desperation Richard bravely threw his grandmother's pasty into the stag's face, but this action enraged the animal even more and before the boy realised what was happening the large red buck had knocked him onto the ground.

The little boy fell flat on his back and the stag, not to forgo the pleasure of a fight, tossed him high into the air with its long, sharp horns.

Again and again, higher and higher, the enraged animal tossed the lad until Richard was left with no more life inside him than a limp rag doll. The stag turned him over and over, yet neither boy nor animal made any noise.

Meanwhile, the farm labourers shouted to four men in a nearby bare telling them to come quickly to save the boy. The farmer's men immediately hurried to the meadow with their pitchforks and a dog, but the stag would not stop goring the body.

The four men poked the stag with their sharp pitchforks,

THE STAG GAVE A MIGHTY ROAR AND ADVANCED MORE QUICKLY

but still could not push the animal away from its victim; and it was only when they set the dog upon the stag that it ran away.

The men gently lifted up Richard's small body —— it had been gored in a most horrible and dreadful manner and there were no signs of life. They carried the little boy to his home; and we can only imagine what happened when his mother came to the door and saw her dead child.

From Riches to Rags

Once upon a time there was a very rich family whose fine residence stood on the top of a hill overlooking the busy sea-port of Falmouth. This wealthy couple had only one son — a handsome, clever, young man whom they idolised.

Suddenly this family was reduced to poverty by an unexpected stroke of bad luck when all their fishing vessels were wrecked during a severe storm in the Bay of Biscay. These ships had been carrying a valuable cargo of pilchards to Spain, but now everything lay at the bottom of the ocean.

The father and mother sold their large house and moved into a humble, little cottage in the village of Penryn, but the son decided to leave home because he did not want to become a burden upon his parents now that they were so poor.

He was determined to travel overseas and make his fortune — for he had heard fascinating stories about finding gold in far-off lands and was determined to succeed in his search for riches. Anxious to repay a debt of gratitude and to make amends for their terrible misfortune, he promised his parents he would soon return to share his fortune.

The son bid a tearful farewell to his loving father and mother and. rode his horse into Falmouth to board a sailing ship for America. However, before leaving that port lie visited his sweetheart — a young and beautiful woman whose father was the local Squire.

Unknown to his

parents, the young couple had been lovers for many months and his sweetheart now faithfully promised to wait for his return, no matter how long he might be away.

A few years passed and the young adventurer wrote home to his elderly parents and to his promised bride until eventually he had collected enough wealth to return to England and marry his sweetheart. Wanting to surprise his parents, he did not tell them of his intentions.

He landed at Falmouth one dark, stormy night and immediately rode horse to Penryn where his love awaited him. The happy couple joyfully flew into each other's arms and he promised to marry her as soon as possible after telling their parents.

He gave his beloved a gold ring and diamond necklace and showed her all the treasures he had brought back from the gold-mines of America. Together they agreed to give his parents a wonderful surprise before announcing their wedding plans.

The young man disguised himself by attaching a black beard to his face and placing a black wig upon his head so that the old couple would not recognise him.

He planned to go to his parents' humble cottage as a stranger and ask for a night's lodging. Then, on the following morning, he intended to reveal himself as their long-lost son.

Bidding his sweetheart farewell, the young man could barely contain his excitement at the thought of the wonderful present he was about to give his parents. He could imagine the look of happiness on their dear, beloved faces.

Although the night was dark and dismal, his heart was full of joy as he trudged towards their cottage carrying under his arm a casket full of gold which he intended to give them with his affection.

Pretending to be a merchant from China, he knocked on their door and begged a lodging for the night, saying he would repay their kindness in the morning.

The poor couple agreed readily and gave him a bowl of bread and milk for supper before showing him upstairs to bed. Later, the mother noticed the fascinating casket which the stranger had forgotten to take upstairs with him; so out of curiosity she lifted the lid and saw the golden treasure within.

She was filled with a great envy and said to herself, "Why is this stranger so rich when we are so poor? Such immense treasure would save us from poverty and shame."

It was this hatred of poverty that made her soul dark with a desperate desire to steal the stranger's gold. Would not this treasure save them from further suffering?

She was determined to have it; so, after making sure that the stranger was asleep, she told her husband about the gold in the casket and urged him to steal it for themselves by murdering the foreigner.

"After all," she said, "no one would notice his disappearance because he is a merchant who travels all around the world."

At first her husband was horrified at such a suggestion and refused to do the dastardly deed; but there is a saying, "Poverty is a foe to virtue" and the husband's scruples were soon overcome.

Since he had agreed to commit the horrible act, soon that ruthless pair were climbing the stairs. They quietly entered the dark room and approached the stranger's bed. They could scarcely make out the sleeping form beneath a blanket, but the mother held up a small candle and by its faint rays the father thrust his knife into the heart of the stranger.

To avoid detection they knew that on the following

morning they must bury their victim in the nearby marshes. It was necessary in order to cover up their cruel deed.

Therefore, long before the sun arose, they carried the stranger's body downstairs, wrapped it in a blanket and placed it in a push-cart. Then they returned indoors to gloat over the gold which now belonged to them.

Next morning they were about to push the cart down to the marshes when a young lady suddenly appeared at the door with a smiling face and happy greetings. She asked the old couple if their son was awake yet.

"You must be mistaken," the mother said, "our son has been overseas for several years and we don't know when he will return."

"Oh, no," the young lady replied, "your son returned home yesterday and wanted to surprise yon with a gift of gold."

The wretched parents rushed outside to the cart and pulled back the blanket that covered the body. They gazed upon the murdered corpse in the light of day, only to discover that it was indeed their only child.

What a catastrophe! What feelings of remorse were present in the hearts and minds of the perpetrators of this dreadful murder?

No punishment, however severe, could possibly compare with the pain and suffering they must have endured at the sudden realisation of what they had done.

POVERTY IS A FOE TO VIRTUE
KILL HIM

THE KNOCKERS

Old Cornish folks were very superstitious people who seriously believed that pixies inhabited the subterranean passages where miners dug for tin and copper. In those days it was customary for a miner to leave a few crumbs on the ground when eating his "croust" (lunch) because this would please the little folk and bring the miner good luck.

But, if a miner failed to leave some crumbs he would be cursed with bad luck. The little pixies who lived deep underground had a special name — they were known as knockers because miners said they could hear them knocking to indicate their presence.

Once upon a time there was a miner working alone in a deep subterranean passage when he heard voices calling out to him. He estimated that the shrill voices came from some distance behind him:-

"*Tom Trevorrow! Tom Trevorrow!*
Leave some of thy fuggan for Bucca,
Or bad luck to thee to-morrow!"

Being very hungry, Tom ignored the request of the little folk and ate all his pasty without leaving a single crumb. To his surprise he heard the knockers again, but this time their voices were very angry:-

"Tommy Trevorrow! Tommy Trevorrow!
We'll send thee bad luck tomorrow,
Thou old curmudgeon to eat all thy fuggan,
And not leave a didjan for Bucca."

Tom was somewhat scared to realise they were furious with him because he had not left a single crumb (a didjan) but a little later he settled down to doze off for a few minutes.

When Tom awoke from his nap, he was terrified to see scores of knockers standing near him in a threatening circle. They were resting on their tools — little, miserable, old, dried-up creatures. The tallest of them was no more than three foot six inches high.

"Tom Trevorrow! Tom Trevorrow!
Leave some of thy fuggan for Bucca,
Or bad luck to thee tomorrow!"

Their legs were as thin as drumsticks and their arms as long, or longer, than their legs. They had big, ugly heads with grey or red locks, squinting eyes, hook noses, and mouths stretching from ear to ear.

They mocked him, distorting their mouths in the most horrible manner, until Tom sprang to his feet and ran back down the tunnel.

Too tired to run any further Tom turned to face his enemies, but when he bravely stood his ground and stared at them they gradually melted away, changing shapes like the curling smoke from a chimney.

Next day, this time accompanied by his son, Tom again went down the mine. On entering the same tunnel he noticed that the timber posts were bulging and ready to give way under the weight of the roof.

So they put in new timber to make the walls secure, as they thought, but the goblins were incessantly knocking to indicate their presence; and all the time Tom was putting in the new posts he could plainly hear them working against him on the other side of the wall.

The longer that Tom worked in this dangerous place the nearer the knockers came towards him until the wall suddenly split open and he felt the ground move beneath his feet.

He yelled to his son to run for the cage and together they

raced down the long tunnel. They fell into the skip just as the walls collapsed behind them and Tom shouted to the winchman to pull them up for dear life.

Despite this narrow escape, Tom and his son still came very near to being killed for just as they stepped out of the cage the rope broke and the machine hurtled backwards down the shaft taking Tom's tin and valuable work-tools with it.

Tom was dismayed to realise that all his labour and time had gone for nothing. Without his tools he could not work and so for weeks afterwards Tom had to live on charity money. When he did return to work in the old mine, the knockers continued tormenting him to such an extent that eventually he returned to his former job as a stone-cutter in Uny Lelant.

THE COPPER MINES OF CAMBORNE SUPPLIED THE WORLD

Those two ancient towns of Redruth and Camborne nowadays have little character and wear a rather forlorn appearance, their days of greatness gone for ever. Yet, about three miles west of these two towns was once the largest copper mine in Cornwall — Dolcooth Mine. It was one mile in length and penetrated by innumerable shafts and many subterranean passages. Its depth was 1,200 feet and in its heyday five engines were kept busy bringing up the ore and rubbish, whilst three more engines kept the mine free from water. Just imagine the unceasing and deafening rattle of eight gigantic engines as thick smoke issued from the deep and dark abyss of the pit. There were 1,600 men, women and children employed at Dolcooth Mine, producing over 70 tons of copper each month for the rich owners. A mine captain (manager) such as my great-grandfather Henry Skewis was paid thirteen guineas a month, whilst his eight subordinate captains earned six guineas per month.

Yet, unhealthy as it may have been down Dolcooth copper mine, it was far better than working in the smelting refinery at Hayle where some of the copper ore was transported to be smelted and then rolled into flat sheets at the pounding house. The ore was smelted and refined through six or seven furnaces, but the appearance of the men who worked there was shocking as the intense heat was very bad for the workers' health. Their emaciated figures were like shadows in front of the flames for they looked like walking corpses.

After only spending a few years in the refinery those workers were laid in their graves. Today, only a ruined building stands at this place known as Copperhouse in memory of its once important role in the production of material to make our kitchen utensils.

Working-class families could not afford a proper headstone in those hard times and the epitaphs found in a country churchyard truly reflect the hard lives of our ancestors who toiled down mines, or in the fields, for a mere pittance.

"The miner dieth and wasteth away. Yea, he giveth up the ghost and where is he?"

"Rest for the toiling hand, rest for the anxious brow. Rest from the weary way, rest from all labours now."

Superstition ruled the lives of the old folks. For example, criminals and suicides were always buried at a crossroads so that their souls could not find the way back to their native village. On Bodmin Moor there can still be seen a mysterious burial mound by the roadside known as "Jay's Grave". The story goes that some time in the 18th. Century, poor Kitty Jay became pregnant out of wedlock and hanged herself in shame.

There is a saying that without pilchards the Cornish folks would have starved to death. Along the rocky coasts of Cornwall great shoals of these fish would arrive without fail each season. In fact, the St. Ives pilchard fishery was the largest in the world. Not only were pilchards the staple diet of the locals, but these fish were also exported to Roman Catholic countries such as Spain, France and Italy. The fish were caught in a long net (a seine) some 1,230 feet long and 84 feet deep. As the season approached a man (called a huer) would be paid half-a-guinea a week to stay in a hut on a high part of the coast to keep watch for the fish. As soon as the huer saw a purple tinge in the water he knew a great shoal of pilchards was coming and so he would shout to warn the local fishermen. As well as pilchards they would also catch a large supply of conger eels. These snake-like fish are enormous with eyes as big as human ones. "What can be done with such a creature?" asked a traveller one day, looking at one that weighed nearly 80 pounds. "Why," replied the fisherman, "cut him up and put him in a pie to be sure — they are good eating, you know." The traveller replied, "I would sooner eat the serpent that tempted Eve in the Garden of Eden."

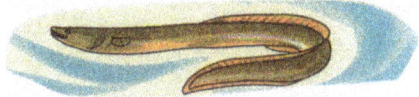

When some mines closed down because competition overseas made the price of tin and copper so low it was just not worth the trouble of mining these ores, then emigration began upon a scale hitherto unprecedented. Deliverance from poverty seemed to be in leaving Cornwall. Thus, by the year 1850, thousands who had never previously even crossed the River Tamar made their escape to North America, the Australian diggings, or round Cape Horn to Chile, or the Californian gold fields; and when many of them sent home tales of wondrous riches, more and more miners followed their example. Many would have heard about the luck of a miner named Hosking who emigrated to the diamond fields of South Africa and found a nugget of gold weighing 4 kgs. Even fishermen began to emigrate, going to the Isle of Guernsey where the famed lobsters were plentiful. Various advertisements appeared daily, appealing for miners to proceed to the Wallaroo Copper mines in South Australia, or to the new silver field opening up near Adelaide; and by the late 1800's all the gold and silver mines in Mexico were being worked by the thousands of Cornish emigrants.

THE CURSING PSALM

In West Cornwall there is a small mining village by the name of St. Gwinear where my parents were married at the end of the First World War. Many of my dead ancestors lie mute in the churchyard there under flattening mounds of earth because poor miners and their families could not afford to have a proper tombstone.

There is a story connected with my parents' village that concerns a lonely place just where the narrow, winding lane crosses a long, straight road. A sign-post stands in the middle of the crossroad. Although it may seem superfluous at this late date to recall such ancient history, a young woman was buried at this very spot sometime in the early 1800's.

This unfortunate creature had become pregnant in consequence of an illicit affair and resolved, in desperation, to put an end to her life.

In those far-off days it was a religious law that any person who committed suicide could not be buried in consecrated ground, nor have a religious funeral service — and this church ruling did not change until the middle of the 19th. century.

Therefore, the custom was to bury a suicide in the middle of the night at the junction of four ways. Sometimes, the actual grave was dug directly beneath a sign-post, but it was most important that the burial party should leave no sign of any disturbance on the ground.

Let me relate the unfortunate circumstances that led to this young woman's suicide. The village of St. Gwinear stands on top of a steep hill and consists of a curving terrace of about thirty houses with an ancient church at one end and an inn at the other.

In those days there were no proper roads so folks walked along lanes with high hedges. Such a lane descended the steep hill to a cluster of tiny, miners' cottages known as the hamlet of Drannock. It was down this grassy way that Thomas Mitchell often walked to visit his sweetheart, a miner's daughter.

Elizabeth was a lovely girl and they were secretly engaged to be married. Unfortunately, one evening after a sharp quarrel over the details of their wedding — and perhaps Elizabeth was most in the wrong here because she kept the knowledge of her expectant child from him — Thomas departed from her in a bad mood and pretended to pay attention to another woman in his village, simply to teach Elizabeth a lesson.

When Thomas did not call upon her for over a week, Elizabeth was broken-hearted and thought that Thomas had definitely left her for another. She would not be comforted by family, or friends, and wept day and night for her lost lover. She had no appetite and was afraid to venture outside the house because she thought people were laughing at her misfortune.

She was unaware that Thomas had been called away from his home on business and therefore was absent from her through no fault of his own.

Feeling utterly forsaken and without hope of ever seeing Thomas on her doorstep again, Elizabeth took a Bible and folded down the page on which was written the 109th. Psalm. She underlined all those verses that describe the various ways in which to curse one's enemy — and then she went out into a field and hanged herself from the bough of an oak tree.

Her lover, Thomas, on returning home that Sunday evening and realising that he had stayed away from Elizabeth for too long, hurried down the hill to her home. He wanted to beg her forgiveness for his foolish behaviour.

Arriving at the tiny cottage, he asked her father if he might speak to Elizabeth, but was told that Elizabeth had not been seen for two or three hours. Suddenly Thomas was filled with a dreadful foreboding and cried out, *"Good heavens, she has destroyed herself!"*

Thomas ran outside and searched the nearby fields, only to find her body hanging from a tree. It was true. She had killed herself, and that night Elizabeth was secretly buried in a grave at the junction of four lanes outside St, Gwinear village.

When her Bible was handed to Thomas, he found Psalm 109 on the turned-down page and read the fearful curses that Elizabeth had underlined: -

Alas, the mouth of the wicked, and the mouth of the deceitful, have spoken against me.
They have spoken against me with a lying tongue.
For my love, he is now my adversary,
And he has rewarded me evil for good,
And hatred for mv love.
Set a wicked man over him,
And let Satan stand at his right hand.
When he shall be judged,
Let him be condemned.
Let his days be few, and let another take his office.
Let his children be fatherless and his wife a widow.

The whole of Psalm 109 is full of similar execrations and is known in churches as 'The Cursing Psalm'. No wonder poor Thomas cried out in agony, *"I am ruined for ever and ever."*

He fled from the village where he had spent so many happy hours as if the place were a nest of scorpions.

He travelled throughout the length and breadth of Cornwall in search of peace, but there was no peace for him anywhere and even Time did not heal his pain. He no longer attended church in case the cursing psalm might be read out.

When he was badly injured at work in a tin-mine, he believed it was due to the effect of the curse for Thomas was now completely under the control of those curses placed upon him by the woman he had loved.

Every unhappy thing that befell him was the result of her dreadful spell hanging over his head. He never slept soundly, for Elizabeth would appear to him in his broken slumbers with a Bible open in her hand — and others in the same house would often hear him cry out aloud in his sleep, *"Oh, Betsy, my dear Betsy, shut the book, shut the book!"*

Eventually, he returned to his home in St. Gwinear and proposed to a young woman, but she was superstitious and refused his offer, saying, *"Do you want the curses of that dead girl upon my head, too?"*

At last Thomas found a girl in another village who, not having heard about his past misfortunes, agreed to marry him. However, on the way to St. Hilary Church for his wedding, a sudden and violent storm overtook his carriage and he could hear Elizabeth's curses in the roaring of the wind and saw the garments of his dead sweetheart in the sheets of lightning.

He covered his eyes and was doubled up with fear and anxiety, but when he reached the gates of the church the storm abated and the sun began to shine again as if the Devil were afraid to enter God's place of worship.

Thomas was a kind husband and made his wife very

happy. Sadly, both their children, a boy and a girl, died at birth; and then, scarcely two years after the marriage, Thomas went to join his beloved children in the churchyard.

However, this tragic story does not quite end there for as Thomas's body lay at rest in St. Hilary Church that infamous 'Cursing Psalm' was read out to the congregation.

Afterwards, the elderly vicar said he could not remember who had told him to include Psalm 109 in the funeral service, yet it was clearly written in his notes.

Coincidence, perhaps? Or was it Elizabeth from the grave, making sure she had the last word?

GRAVE WORDS

In Cornish churchyards one may still find on a very old headstone the following epitaph. It expresses the feelings of a worn-out housewife.

> Here lies a poor woman who was always tired, For she lived In a house where help was not hired. Her last words on earth were, "Dear friends, I am going Where washing ain't done, nor sweeping, nor sewing. And everything there is exact to my wishes, For where they don't eat there's no washing of dishes. Don't mourn for me now! Don't mourn for me never! I'm going to do nothing for ever and ever!"

MEMORIAL TO JOHN WESLEY AT GWENNAP-PIT {near Redruth}

ZENNOR – A CORNISH VILLAGE

Zennor is a small village situated in the far west of Cornwall, not far from Land's End. In this area the visitor will find pre-history in the forms of granite outcrops, burial chambers and stone circles. There is a megalithic stone tomb not far from this isolated fishing village.

Zennor's church dates back to the 6th. Century when Celtic missionaries first arrived here, but the present building dates back to the 12th. Century. You can find a list of vicars dating back to 1270.

The little church is dedicated to St. Senera who came from Brittany. But most tourists come here to see the Zennor mermaid. On a bench-end inside the church you can see the carved figure of a mermaid. The story goes that the mermaid attended church on several Sundays in order to capture the interest of a member of the church choir.

Matthew Trewhella was well-known for his fine tenor voice and he had noticed the fair-haired young lady seated by the back of the church, so one Sunday he slipped out the back door and followed her a mile or so down to the coast. She beckoned to him and he followed her into the sea at Pendour Cove — and he was never seen again.

Many years later as a ship pulled into the Cove its captain heard a woman's voice calling for Matthew Trewhella. Looking down at a rock he caught sight of a mermaid as she disappeared beneath the waves.

THE MERMAID OF ZENNOR

Today, many tourists visit Zennor in the hope that they, too, might catch sight of that famous mermaid swimming near the shore. They visit the church to see the carved oak bench.

Zennor Village

Zennor Church

Pendour Cove

Ancient carved bench ends in St. Sennara Church, Zennor.

Bridge On Bodmin Moor

"White Hart" Inn, Inagvan Village

Lands End

Foot of England

DETECTED BY A DREAM

Sometimes innocent Cornish maidens believed that seduction would lead to marriage; but, sadly, in most cases women were left literally holding the baby when their lovers decamped. The moral, if there be any, to my following story is that young women should keep their wits about them.

It was in the year 1826 that a young girl named Mary Marten found she was expecting a child and, naturally, her angry father demanded to know the name of her lover. When Mary confessed that his name was William Corder, the son of a neighbouring farmer, her father almost exploded with rage.

"Well, maid, he had better marry thee, or I'll take a gun to him," threatened her father, "I want no bastard child in this family!"

Fearful for his life, William Corder promised Mr. Martin he would marry Mary in Bodmin Town; but after she left home her worried parents never saw or heard from her again.

In the meantime, William Corder advertised for a wife in both the *'Morning Herald'* and the *'Sunday Times'* and received no fewer than sixty replies from a variety of women, all eagerly searching for a husband. He selected a wealthy widow who ran a school for young ladies in Brentford.

Now, after several months Mary's worried mother began to have strange dreams in which she saw her daughter standing inside their red barn. In another dream she saw her daughter being murdered.

Mary's father, at the repeated suggestion of his wife, dug up the floor of the barn and found a corpse beneath the dry earth. Although it was several weeks since her disappearance, he immediately recognised the remains of his only daughter.

Her face was covered with dark blood which had issued from the mouth and around the throat were terrible bruises and impressions of fingers. The arms were bent over on the chest and were rigid; and on both wrists were deep and circular impressions of a rope.

Finally, the distraught father noticed how the flesh of Mary's neck was much swollen and on closer examination found a piece of lace tied so tightly round the throat that it was almost hidden from view. The state of poor Mary's dress indicated that this strip of material had been roughly torn from the front of her bodice.

It was obvious to the police that Mary had been subjected to a brutal and vicious attack and immediately they began looking for her dangerous killer. When Mary's mother was asked if she recognised the man in her dreams she replied in no uncertain manner, "I tell e t'was William Corder."

HE KILLED MARY IN THE RED BARN

The search for his whereabouts began and after a few weeks of intense investigation Corder was arrested, tried and found guilty of Mary's murder. However, the unique aspect of this case is the fact that while in prison William Corder wrote a confession in the form of a poem; and after he was hanged outside Bury St. Edmund's Gaol on the 11th. August, 1828, his poem was printed as a street-ballad and sold over one-and-a-half million copies.

As was the custom in those days, the body of a hanged murderer was used for anatomical purposes — and so William Corder's skeleton can still be seen in the museum of the College of Surgeons in London.

Come— all you bold young thoughtless men, A warn-ing take by me;

THE BALLAD OF MARY MARTEN — WRITTEN BY HER MURDERER

"My name is William Corder, the Truth I do declare,
I courted Mary Marten, most beautiful and fair.
I promised that I'd marry her, all on a summer's day,
Instead of that I was resolved to take her life away.
I went into her father's house upon the eighth of May,
I said, "O come, my dearest one, we'll fix the wedding day.
If you will meet me at Red Barn, as sure as I have life,
I'll take you down to Bodmin Town and there make you my wife."
I went straight home to fetch my gun, my pick-axe and my spade;
I went into the big Red Barn and there I dug her grave.
With heart so light she thought no harm, to meet me she did go,
But I killed her in that big Red Barn and laid her body low.

Her mother had a dreadful dream, she dreamed it three nights o'er;
She dreamed that her dear daughter lay beneath the Red Barn floor.
So her husband went into the barn and in the ground he thrust,
And there he found his daughter dear lay mingling with the dust.
Come listen, you young thoughtless men, take pity now on me,
For Monday next will be my last as I hang upon the tree."

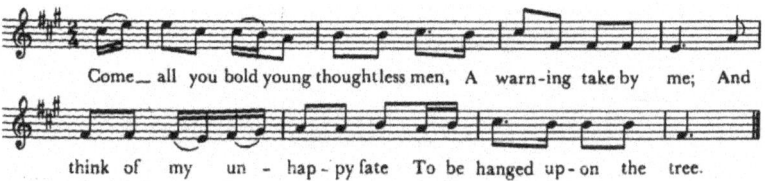

POISONING

Even in our modern times, as many as eight children a day receive medical treatment after swallowing toxic substances. Statistics tell us that 3,000 children under the age of four, each year in Victoria (Australia) require urgent medical assistance after ingesting poisonous products at home.

Today, thanks to speedy, effective treatment, children's lives are saved, but in 1871 such help was not available to a little Cornish girl named Emma Mitchell.

The child's grandmother was the only member of the family that seemed able to explain the unfortunate chain of events leading up to Emma's tragic death. Here is the evidence she gave at the Inquest:

"My son's house was over-run with mice and so he bought a small quantity of arsenic to destroy the nasty vermin. My daughter-in-law, Maud, last night spread a small amount of arsenic on some bread and butter and after the children had gone to bed, laid it

down on the threshold of my bedroom door. It was laid there to poison the mice who were running in and out of my room.

The next morning the chimney-sweep came earlier than usual so Maud was in a real muddle for she had not prepared the rooms. My little grand-daughter slept in the same bed-chamber with me and she must have got up early while her mother was still downstairs with the sweep. When I got out of bed I looked for the bread and butter spread with arsenic — but it had gone, so I thought the mice must have taken it. I told Maud and she asked 4-year old Elizabeth if she had seen it.

Elizabeth said she had given it to her baby sister, Emma, to stop her crying. Of course, my daughter-in-law was alarmed and went to the village shop to get some antimony wine as an emetic. Maud gave it to the child who was then sick. Maud then gave the child some castor oil, but the child only got worse and died that evening."

THE WAYWARD HAT

The landscape of West Cornwall is ugly, bleak and melancholy due to hideous scars from many centuries of tin and copper mining. The countryside of my forebears was destroyed and turned into a barren waste by greedy mine owners.

Today, as fierce Atlantic gales sweep across this narrow peninsula, an eerie whistling echoes inside the hollow brick chimneys of crumbling engine houses. The wind blows down disused mine shafts through rotten timbers and narrow tunnels into underground caverns which are ruinous now and full of water.

Ancestors rest from their labours under moss-covered mounds in village churchyards — and as one of their tombstones aptly says: -

Don't mourn for me now,
Don't mourn for me never;
I'm going to do nothing
For ever and ever."

It is a heartfelt cry from the grave to give us some idea of the hard work and sufferings they endured during those hard times.

By the 1860's, mining came to an end in Cornwall and there was a great emigration of the population to seek work and opportunities across the sea in countries such as Australia, Chile, California, New Zealand and the United States.

However, when the hundreds of mines were closed down, unfortunately nothing was down to make these places safe for the local inhabitants — and so they daily faced the danger of open shafts close to their roads and dwelling places.

One of my Skewis ancestors fell down a shaft while walking home one night between Redruth and St. Day. The local newspaper records his death and adds: *"No less than 18 lives have been lost at Gwennap where open shafts are everywhere."* Then the newspaper adds an ominous thought: *"How many of these open mine shafts have become the means of suicide, murder, or accidental deaths; no one will ever know?"*

My great-grandfather, Captain Thomas Moyle, worked at the Wheal Gerry copper mine (Camborne) until his death in 1827 and was probably its last mine agent; and by the middle of the nineteenth century Wheal Gerry was nothing more than a ghostly area of ruined miners' houses and abandoned mine shafts.

One Sunday in the year 1871, Jack Hocking, a young farm labourer, was walking across Wheal Gerry when a strong gust of wind snatched the hat from his head and sent it flying into the air.

Immediately Jack gave chase for it was his father's best hat which he had borrowed to wear to chapel that morning — and he knew his father would be very angry if anything happened to it.

Each time Jack reached out to grab the wayward hat it seemed to rise up on invisible wings and float tantalisingly above his head. Then it would drift away over the prickly gorse bushes that covered this former copper-mine.

Jack followed the hat until it suddenly vanished from his sight down a deep hole in the ground. Filled with dismay, Jack stared into that dark abyss and gave up any hopes of retrieving his father's best hat.

He was about to turn away in despair when suddenly he

caught sight of that hat, about a hundred feet down, snagged on a rotten piece of timber.

At that moment, Jack noticed a stout boy walking towards him and suddenly a brilliant plan began to form in his head.

"Hey, boy, come over here!" shouted Jack.

"What d'ya want?" asked the stout boy, in a sullen voice, as he cautiously approached the edge of the shaft where Jack was standing.

"I'll give you a penny if you can find a long rope and bring it here," said Jack.

Off ran the boy as fast as his fat legs could carry him — and soon he returned with the desired item.

"Where's my penny?" he asked, before handing it over.

Jack took a coin from his pocket and placed it in the boy's outstretched, grubby hand. "Now, boy, you can have another penny if you help me to recover my hat. It's down this old mine shaft."

"I'm not climbing down there to rescue your hat. Ma would kill me if I got my best clothes dirty," replied the boy.

"Don't worry," said Jack, "I only want you to hold this rope while I climb down. If you tie it around your waist and lie down I'm sure you can support my weight."

Holding the rope around his waist, the stout boy watched while Jack slowly lowered himself over the top of the pit and slid down the rope. The fat boy's heavy body was as firm as a tree-trunk.

At last, Jack reached the wayward hat and tucked it safely inside his shirt.

"Look out, I'm coming up!" he yelled to the stout boy as he started climbing the rope. However, just as Jack put his right hand over the top of the shaft, the stout boy's concentration

was broken by the arrival of a man who said his mother wanted him immediately.

The stout boy nervously stood up and spoke to the man, but as he did so he carelessly let the rope slip from his grasp. Thus before Jack could safely clamber out of that deep pit, the loosened rope caused him to lose his balance and fall backwards.

With a frightened cry, Jack turned several somersaults before hitting the bottom of the shaft. His head was completely smashed in — and when they eventually brought his mangled body to the surface poor Jack lay in agony for five hours before kindly Death brought an end to his suffering.

It was a terrible accident that could have been avoided if only the stout boy had kept his mind on what he was doing. Maybe there's a lesson in this story for all of us.

TRANSPORTATION FOR MACHINE BREAKERS

By the middle of the nineteenth century the application of machinery to farm work was beginning to have a drastic effect upon village labourers. The gradual introduction of machines for ploughing, reaping and thrashing was the beginning of the end for thousands of farm workers. For example, in the past at harvest-time, a farmer needed many workers to thrash his corn because they had to use flails (a manual device consisting of a long, wooden handle with a shorter, free-swinging stick attached to its end).

So now that a machine can replace humans, what will happen to all those agricultural labourers? There is a sad story about a Cornish farmer and his workers which aptly illustrates the tragedy of this agricultural revolution in British History.

Farmer Eustace acquired a modern thrashing machine and consequently sacked several of his farm workers. His new chaff-cutter was a labour saving invention, too. Of course, he always locked his machines away safely inside his big barn each night because he had heard terrible rumours in the village that some of his workers were protesting at losing their jobs and consequently had vowed to destroy his machines. However, Farmer Eustace simply laughed at such silly threats.

Anyway, an Act had just been passed making machine-breaking punishable by death, therefore Farmer Eustace felt quite safe from the vicious threats of any trouble-makers. Still, to make sure his expensive machines were safe he always carefully locked his barn door before going to bed each night.

It was a wise man who once said, "Poverty drives men to desperate deeds" and so it happened one evening in the bar of the Royal Standard Inn that Thomas Trewartha and his friend, James Lugg, met together with several other agricultural labourers who had lost their jobs because of the new farming machinery.

"We must smash those machines to pieces — and it must be done tonight," urged Thomas, "are you a bunch of lily-livered cowards? I tell you, 'tis the only way to get our jobs back. Old Eustace will be helpless without his machinery and 'tis harvest-time soon. Without his new thrashing machine he'll have to give us our jobs back."

"That be right," said James, "don't be afraid, brothers. It's far worse to see your family crying with hunger. Do you want your wife and children to end up in the workhouse? Come on, let's do it tonight!"

The innkeeper, fearing for his safety, ordered the angry mob to leave the premises; so these angry men went outside and began to assemble on the Village Green. Carrying flaming torches and making angry murmurings, they marched in an unruly manner towards the farm of Farmer Eustace.

What happened afterwards on that terrible night is revealed in the subsequent court proceedings held at the

Special Assizes in Bodmin, on Tuesday, 10th. January, 1831, when the case was clearly proved against those "Machine Breakers".

Thomas Trewartha, James Lugg, Jimmy Rowe, Henry Simmonds and Dennis Scone were charged with assembling a riotous crowd to destroy a thrashing machine, the property of George Eustace, of Henver Farm.

Farmer Eustace, in his evidence, told how a mob — of which the prisoners in the dock formed the leading part — came to his house and told him they were there to break his thrashing machine, but if he gave them money and beer they would go away peaceably.

"So I gave them ten shillings and some beer, but they were not content with that and still demanded the keys of my barn. I refused to give them up so they said they would break down the door. They went to my barn and began beating on it. I thought they would smash up my barn, so I went and unlocked the door. They rushed inside and smashed the machine to pieces with their iron bars.

I tried to protect my chaff cutter by standing in front of it, but Rowe held his axe to my head and yelled, 'Damn your eyes, get out of my way or I'll hew you too.'

I swear that all the prisoners standing in the dock were inside my barn on that terrible night. The mob then went into a field and destroyed another machine out there, as well as a machine standing in a shed in the same field."

After the testimony of Farmer Eustace, a villager named William Rodda was called to give evidence and he said, *"I was at Farmer Eustace's place on the 22nd November. I saw Thomas Trewartha and James Lugg in the barn breaking the thrashing-machine; and afterwards I saw Jimmy Rowe smashing up the chaff-cutter in the yard. I also saw Simmonds, Rowe and Scone in front of Farmer Eustace's house. They then went away in a body to the field."*

William Rodda was recalled to the stand later and when asked to reply on oath said, *"I know Jimmy Rowe well and it was definitely him who held the axe over the farmer's head."*

George Harvey, a bricklayer, spoke in favour of Henry Simmonds saying that he had always been a steady and quiet employee; whilst Farmer Blake spoke in favour of Dennis Scone saying that he was a hard-working and reliable shepherd.

However, the Jury found all the prisoners 'GUILTY' and Mr. Justice Pollard then proceeded to pass sentence upon them.

"You, Thomas Trewartha; you, James Lugg, your case leaves the Court without any doubt of your guilt. You, James Rowe, have been convicted of this offence after making a brutal threat upon the prosecutor, which might, but for the intervention of those around you, have ended in murder. It was you, as well as Trewartha and Lugg, who made a demand for money and beer and in consequence of your vicious threats in demanding it, you received it.

You are therefore guilty of an offence, which in the eye of the law, amounts almost to robbery. It is not to be tolerated that men like you should go about with mobs and demand money of those you know to be defenceless. How can any of the true men of this realm enjoy the privacy and tranquillity of his home in safety, if he is to be assaulted after nightfall by riotous and tumultuous mobs, and told that they will not go away unless their demands for money are complied with.

Even after the prosecutor had met your demands, you did not keep faith with him. Did you not say that if he gave you money and beer you would not break his machine? And yet afterwards when you received his money, you still went and broke it?

I hope that this will be a warning to others not to comply with such demands when they are made upon them; for they can be sure that those who make such demands will go on to the accomplishment of the mischief which they originally intended. I hope that the facts of this case will be a warning, which will teach others to resist in the first place — for resistance is the only way to secure the safety of one's property.

As to you, Thomas Trewartha and James Lugg, I can give you no hope of remaining in this country. But you, Dennis Scone, are a shepherd; and you, Henry Simmonds, are a bricklayer's labourer. You have nothing to do with thrashing machines. They do not interfere with your labour and you could not, even in the darkness of your ignorance, suppose that their destruction would do you any good. You will now find, that though you might triumph for a short time, the arm of the law is too strong for you. I hope that your fate will be a warning to others.

You will leave this country, all of you; you will see your friends and relations no more; for though you will be transported for seven years only, it is not likely that at the end of that term you will find yourself in a situation to return. You will remain in a distant land — and the land which you have disgraced will see you no more. Your families will see you no more and will be parted from you for ever in this world.

It is a melancholy and painful duty that I have discharged in passing sentence upon you, but it is a duty which we owe to the public and discharge it we must. The sentence of the Court is that you, Thomas Trewartha; you, James Lugg; you, James Rowe; you, Henry Simmonds; and you, Dennis Scone, be transported beyond the seas to such places as His

Majesty's Privy Council shall think proper; and you will find that this sentence will shortly be carried into effect.

Let this case be a warning to other thrashers who think that these machines are detrimental to them. Be assured that your labour cannot be ultimately hurt by the employment of these machines. If they are profitable to the farmer, they will also be profitable ultimately to the labourer, though they may for a time injure him. If they are not profitable to the farmer, he will soon cease to employ them."

TRANSPORTATION FOR BURGLARY

In 1827 a man and his wife were arrested for breaking into the shop of John Roberts, at Truro, and stealing twelve pounds in copper coins. Elizabeth and Richard Hampton were tried at Cornwall County Assizes though both were imprisoned in Bodmin Gaol for many months while awaiting the trial.

Mr. Huddlestone conducted the case for the prosecution and Mr. Meteyard defended the prisoners, but undoubtedly the evidence seemed to weigh heavily against them.

Police-Constable Trewin took the stand and swore with his hand on the Bible that he would 'tell the Truth, the whole Truth and nothing but the Truth, so help me God'. He said:-

"I was walking my beat on the night in question (May 27th) and as I passed along Boscowen Street I noticed that a side door leading into a shop was slightly ajar. I immediately knocked on the front door to arouse the family. When the owner, Mr. Roberts, came downstairs he discovered that the lock on the door had been broken. He told me he had locked up the shop as usual that evening. Then I entered the shop with Mr. Roberts who looked inside his till and noticed that ten or twelve shillings in loose copper had been taken.

He then went to his desk beside the till and told me that twelve pounds in copper had also gone. All this copper had been counted and tied up in separate packets, each one holding five shillings' worth of copper. He told me that the drawer of the till containing the money was also missing."

A shop-assistant, a young lad named Johnny Phillips, swore on oath that he saw the male prisoner that same evening in the shop and especially noticed him looking at the door.

The next witness was a pawnbroker named Mr. Read who testified that the female prisoner came into his shop on the evening of the 27th. May to redeem various articles of clothing for which she paid about twenty shillings — and more than ten shillings of it was in copper. "When I asked her where she had obtained all the copper, she accounted for it by saying it was her wages. Amongst the copper she gave me, I noticed a piece of starch paper stuck to a penny, as well as a peculiar-looking penny and halfpenny."

These particular coins were shown to the Jury and later identified by the shop assistant as being amongst the copper which he took from a customer on the day of the 26th. May.

Inspector Codd then entered the witness box to give evidence and said, "When I took the female prisoner into custody at the local police station and charged her with the robbery at John Roberts' shop, she said the reason she had so much copper was because she had given half-a-sovereign in change for some copper to a man in the market-place who looked like a sailor, but whom she did not know."

The Police-Inspector continued his evidence, saying, "When I searched the male prisoner I found in his pocket a piece of paper resembling that used by shopkeepers to hold five shillings' worth of copper. We found the drawer of the shop's till in a field nearby."

Mr. Meteyard, in defence of the prisoners, submitted to the Jury that the evidence against the male prisoner was not sufficient to find him guilty.

The learned judge then summed up the whole of the evidence to the Jury; and shortly afterwards the twelve men announced their verdict: "The evidence against the male prisoner was not strong enough and so we find him 'Not Guilty'. But the evidence against the female prisoner is too strong to be ignored, and thus we find her 'Guilty' of the robbery at Robert's shop."

Then his Lordship, in his usual grave and impressive manner, sentenced Elizabeth Hampton to be transported for the term of ten years.

Her last glimpse of home as the convict ship sails past Cornwall

THE CORNISH IN AMERICA
JOHN SKEWES

(Many of my Skewes ancestors who were miners went to America looking for work when the Cornish mines began to close down because of overseas competition. The following two stories describe the kind of dangers many of these miners faced in that foreign land known as "The Wild West".)

On the west coast of America lies Virginia City, a popular area where the Cornish settled in their endless search for gold. From time to time physical weakness, nervous exhaustion and economic anxiety all produced the strains and stresses that often made men's behaviour unpredictable.

On Saturday 19th. December, 1874, four miners sat around a table in the barroom of the Washington House in Virginia City playing their usual game of pedro — Thomas Trembath, Joseph Hodges, Michael Roach and JOHN SKEWES.

About midnight they were joined by Alfred Rule, originally from Camborne, who suggested they should play for drinks instead of just 'for pastime'. This was a grave mistake as it happened, for it made them quarrelsome.

A local newspaper, *"The Virginia City Territorial Enterprise"*, devoted its Editorial to the event on Wednesday, 23rd. December, 1874, as quoted below: -

On Saturday last, in this city, two men, both bearing the reputation of being steady, peaceable and hard-working men, were engaged in a trifling game of cards, when one called the other a liar; a few words followed; a scuffle; and then one shot the other dead. So little is life prized here that the tragedy is now well-forgotten except among the acquaintances of the two actors in the tragedy. And yet it is none the less terrible: and it is time that here in Virginia, with our city government and police, our country government with its courts and sheriffs, with our churches and clergymen, with our schools filled with innocent children; it is time, we repeat, that these causeless murders should cease. To stop an effect we must find and stop the cause. There are two causes in this homicide. The first was the practice, so prevalent here, of carrying weapons.

The participants in the affair were Cornishmen and Cornishmen often have disputes and often engage in fisticuffs. They cannot very well help it. That disposition has been transmitted down through their forefathers for two score generations. A little row, a punch in the head, or a black eye, are simply matters of course with them. But not murder. They shrink from that as shocked and loathingly as any people.

But one of these people had a pistol in his pocket, as has almost everybody else in Virginia. This was the first cause of what resulted in an untimely death. The second cause is that inexplicable but almost universal disposition of people here to say, if a man does not resent an insult, he is a coward; and if he does and slays a fellow man, he is a murderer. In this we are all in part to blame for the killing of Rule. When Rule called Skewes a liar, Skewes was not much shocked, nor much angry. Had there been none present but the two, there is every reason to think nothing more would have come of it, and by the next day the men would have been drinking together again. But Skewes had a friend who advised him that he ought not to let the insult pass without redress, and while the friend advised, Skewes felt the pistol warm in his pocket, and in five minutes the result was a dead man lying on the floor, and another with his peace of mind gone forever, and with a felon's cell opening before him.

The law ought to forbid the carrying of concealed weapons, and the officers ought to mercilessly execute the law. Then our wealthy men ought from their abundance to provide a hall with books, periodicals, daily papers and other innocent attractions, to lure miners form the groggeries, which are now too often their places of resort. It would be but a trifle for our rich men to do, but it would be the commencement of the saving of human life in our midst.

The Four Miners

RULE SHOUTED, "I TAKE NOTHING BACK!
YOU'RE A CHEAT AND A LIAR!"

SKEWES REPLIED, "IF YOU DON'T TAKE BACK YOUR ACCUSATIONS, I'LL KILL YOU!"

DEATH OF A CORNISHMAN IN NICARAGUA

(The local Camborne newspaper reported a shocking occurrence which took place in Nicaragua, Central America, where a Cornishman, named JAMES HENRY SKEWES, a native of the Lizard and for many years a resident of Camborne, lost his life under the most painful circumstances.)

It appears that on Sunday, 24th. May, 1885, Skewes who was employed as foreman-carpenter of the Chontales Mines, was invited by the doctor of the company to go with him on a visit to a patient who resided some fifteen or twenty miles distant — and not having been out of the mines for many months Skewes consented.

On their way back they called at the Company's farm

where they found one of the underground agents, Captain James White (from St. Ives) and a miner, both of whom had been drinking rather freely during the day. Refusing the invitation to drink also, the doctor and Skewes rode homewards, accompanied by Captain White and his companion. The latter, being exceedingly intoxicated, very soon lagged behind the rest at a considerable distance, and on Skewes pointing out the danger of the man being left behind to take care of himself in such a locality, White became annoyed and after a few angry words he rode up to Skewes and struck him a severe blow with his fist.

In self-defence the latter dismounted and upon White repeating his attack, Skewes being a fine stalwart man about thirty years of age, soon got the better of the encounter, knocking his antagonist down two or three times. White who was also a big, powerful man and of a violent overbearing disposition, became so enraged that he drew out his revolver and with an oath placed it close to Skewes and fired. The ball penetrated the right breast and perforated the lung, causing internal hemorrhage which resulted in death within half-an-hour after the wound was received. The doctor gave the alarm as soon as possible and the body was removed to the mines for interment, White being placed in prison. The unfortunate deceased was universally liked and respected at the mines, by natives as well as the English and it was with great difficulty that his murderer escaped being 'lynched'. The company's secretary wrote to his widow, 'I feel deeply for your position and having known Skewes at the mines can bear testimony to the loss we suffer in the death of so good a workman'. White was sentenced to be hanged, but died from the yellow fever before the execution.

JAMES WHITE was not executed because he died from yellow fever which was prevalent in the area at the time. Was it a worse punishment for this murderer than hanging? Yellow fever is an acute disease found in tropical areas and caused by a virus transmitted by mosquitoes — the victim's skin turns yellow and there is a dark-coloured vomit resulting from hemorrhages. (I think hanging would be quicker and less painful.)

MINE CHIMNEY and MINER

SOCIETY AND SUPERSTITION

The desolate countryside in far West Cornwall (where once tin and copper mines were quite prolific) can be a dangerous place to walk upon after heavy rains. Underneath your feet is a honeycomb of hundreds of miles of passages and some of the open shafts can go down as much as 2,000 feet — so take one false step upon the soft, wet ground and you can be plunged instantly into black, hot silence.

Motor-cars have made the greatest changes to the Cornwall I once loved. Roads and lanes have been widened and even cottages removed to make way for car-parks. Petrol stations now occupy the most prominent corners of towns and everywhere huge hoardings have been erected to attract the tourist and his money. In summertime, motor-cars pulling caravans, or boat-trailers, block those quaint little lanes never intended for such heavy traffic. Although the coastline has largely been rescued by the National Trust, most of Cornwall's ancient, beautiful and unspoilt places can only be found by walking. Fortunately, no-one has yet discovered how to build holiday-cabins on the sea.

The Cornish open range in a tiny Cornish kitchen was warming, psychologically as well as physically, especially when heavy rains beat loudly upon the slate roof and poured down the outside pipe into a large wooden water-butt that stood close by the back-door. An iron pot filled with stew bubbled gently on the hob, for the Cornish used to say, "A stew boiled is a stew spoiled". We have come a long way from that old, black range with its coal fire — and when chicken was a once-a-year treat on Christmas Day.

SOCIETY AND SUPERSTITION

It is ironic that the production of children these days should be considered undesirable. In the olden days there were plenty of large families in all the Cornish hamlets and village. Both my grandfathers had twelve siblings and large families were considered quite normal in the 19th Century.

There's the story of a Squire's wife, a would-be philanthropic lady, who visited the humble cottage of a farm-labourer and scolded the wife for just giving birth to her 15th. child. After a while, the poor labourer's wife turned on her and said, "Lor, Miss, that's all the pleasure me an' my old man get."

The Cornish had many superstitions. For example, they believed that 'pixies' were the spirits of infants who had died before baptism and therefore were not allowed to be buried inside the churchyard, but outside the wall instead.

As a child collecting blackberries in the autumn, I was often stung by wild nettles growing in the hedges. The old cure for the pain of nettle stings is to pick a dock-leaf (which always grows next to nettles) and rub it onto the affected areas. The old folks used many natural cures and not only were plants used but also creepy-crawlies. As a small child, I can remember my elderly cousin putting a clean cobweb over the cut on my finger to heal it. In Shakespeare's play (A Midsummer Night's Dream) Bottom says to Fairy Cobweb, "I shall desire of you more acquaintance; if I cut my finger I shall make bold with you."

A girl who wished to have a vision of her future husband would recite the following charm on the evening of the first Friday in the month: — *"On Friday night I go to bed, a threefold apron neath my head. In my bed I wish to sleep, in my sleep I wish to dream. In my dream I wish to see who my true love is to be. Let him come by sea, or land, let him by my bedside stand. Let him be in best array, or come in clothes he wears each day."*

THE WORST SHIPWRECK
IN CORNISH HISTORY

During the reign of Queen Anne (1702-14) the English nation was involved with several wars against the French and also what is usually called the War of the Spanish Succession. It was the English navy that proved capable of defeating those enemies with its fine ships and brave sailors. However, in 1707 a distinguished British Admiral, Sir Cloudesley Shovell, was returning at the head of his fleet from foreign service, when his ship was wrecked, with several other ships, and almost 2,000 men were lost.

Admiral Shovell and his brave companions met their sad fate on the rocks of the Scilly Isles — and the only particulars about his shipwreck can be found in the Museum on St. Mary's Island. If this tragedy had occurred in modern times the whole world would have heard about it through newspapers and television, but there is no written record of that lamentable shipwreck in 1707, except for some oral information from a few locals and the evidence of a sole survivor.

It is said that some of the bodies cast up on the shore were buried on the isle of St. Mary's and these included Admiral Shovell's two stepsons and his pet greyhound.

History books tell us that Sir Cloudesley Shovell (1650-1707) was born to poor parents in a Norfolk village and as a young boy he was apprenticed to a shoemaker, but soon ran away to sea. He started his naval career as a cabin-boy and rose through the ranks. He very early distinguished himself and showed a remarkable ability while working on various ships and soon was promoted to the rank of lieutenant. While on duty in the Mediterranean in 1674 he captured and burnt four pirate ships at Tripoli. Then in 1689 he was promoted to the rank of Commander and helped to defeat the French who were trying to land in Ireland at Bantry Bay (Cork). He was knighted by Queen Anne for his services. In 1692 he supported Admiral Russell at La Hague and burned 20 of the enemy ships. He helped in the capture of Barcelona (Spain) and also took part in the siege of Toulon in 1707 where his men nearly destroyed the town and burnt eight of the enemy's ships of war in the harbour.

Sir Cloudesley Shovell left a squadron of thirteen ships in the Mediterranean to continue service against the Spanish while he was returning home with the rest of his fleet. He sailed from Gibraltar on October 10th. with fifteen battle-ships, five smaller ships and yacht. The Admiral's ship, the 'Association', had a crew of 900. Three ships of his fleet which closely followed him (and were also wrecked) were the 'Eagle', the 'Romney' and the 'Firebrand' — so the total number of lives lost could not have been fewer than two thousand.

It was on the 21st. October, 1707, when they believed that the English Channel had opened before them, but the night was dark and the wind had increased to a gale with squalls and heavy rain. On the following day the same dark rainy weather hid from their sight the lighthouse of Scilly and it was too late by the time they noticed rocks on both sides of the ship.

On the 31st. October, there was news that the body of Sir Cloudesley Shovell had been found on the Coast of Cornwall by a fisherman who was searching among the rocks. He took a tin box out of one of the carcasses that was floating around and found in it the name of Admiral Shovell. The corpse had no other identification because the clothes had been washed away by the rough waves. In those days there was no medical means of identification, so the body was taken to Plymouth to be embalmed and then carried to London to be buried in Westminster Abbey.

Were these the true facts about the Admiral's death? Or do we believe the story that many years later a terrible confession was made by a dying woman to a clergyman on St. Mary's island? She said that the Admiral had been washed ashore near her cottage on the island and that he was weak but still alive. She said that she murdered him with a brutal hit to his head and stole the valuables he had upon him. She gave the emerald ring that had been on his finger to the minister as she lay dying. She said that she had been afraid to sell it lest it would lead to the discovery of her guilt, adding that she could not die in peace until she had made this full confession.

On The Rocks

The rocky coastline of Cornwall cause many Shipwrecks

SOCIAL CONDITIONS

Cornish folks are fond of pies and pasties; indeed, there is a saying that if a Cornishman were to catch the Devil he would put him in a pie, or pasty.

Years ago a hungry stranger entered a Cornish village inn and the landlord offered him Tammy pie' which he ate heartily and enjoyed very much. Next morning, the traveller consumed the rest of the pie with great enjoyment.

"How did you like the mistress's 'lammy pie'?" inquired the innkeeper as the stranger was about to depart.

"It was excellent," replied the stranger, "the best lamb I ever tasted."

"Lord, bless you," exclaimed the innkeeper, "it was not that. 'Lammy pie' is not made of lamb."

"Well, what the devil is it made of then?" exclaimed the horrified traveller.

"Why, our poor kiddy, to be sure," said the landlord, "who died yesterday of the shab." And to comfort the stranger, he added, "Oh, don't worry; our pet goat only died from a skin complaint which is quite common in kids.

Now, you may think that the 'foot-and-mouth' disease which spread throughout Great Britain during 2001 is a modem cattle plague. On the contrary, this same cattle plague was wide-spread throughout Cornwall during the 19th. Century and in the year 1865 we read that the worst affected farms were in the Truro and Padstow areas. A 'cordon sanitaire' was thrown around each infected district to prevent any movement of animals, offal, hides and fodder.

However, farmers themselves often broke these health regulations and so the disease continued. To stop the spread of 'foot-and-mouth', days of fasting and prayer were held in many towns throughout Cornwall and the people prayed continually to God to take away this terrible curse that had fallen upon their animals.

The old Cornish folks made great use of the wild herbs that grow freely in the hedgerows and along the cliff-tops. They used Samphire (the herb of St. Peter) for pickling which is a cliff-top plant with salty, fleshy leaves. Do not confuse it with the poisonous Hemlock which also grows in profusion in the hedgerows. Now, in the year 1861 an Italian boat was moored in Falmouth harbour and two of the sailors bought some oysters at the quayside. Then they thought they would go into the nearby fields and find some turnips and herbs to cook with their shellfish. The two men pulled up some turnips and then began to gather some of the juicy-looking green plants growing in the hedge, chewing upon them at the same time. After about ten minutes Rossi fell down and began to howl with pain. About ten minutes later his mate, Bonich, fell down in the same way, so neither man was able to speak to the farm-labourers who rushed to their aid, but it was obvious to any onlooker that those two sailors were suffering from excruciating pains in the stomach. One sailor managed to point to the bunch of herbs he was holding in his hand, as the foam came out of his mouth and the sweat poured down his face. Thus, the farm-labourers realised that the two foreigners had eaten Hemlock, mistaking it for Samphire; but there was no medical help available to save them from a cruel and violent death. So, may their untimely and painful end be a warning to all visitors who enter the county of Cornwall and wish to sample its wild herbs.

SOCIAL CONDITIONS

By the middle of the 19th.Century Cornish miners were scattered all over the face of the earth from Arizona to Africa. They used to say that wherever there was a hole in the ground you would find a Comishman at the bottom of it. Though Cornish mining is now a thing of the past, the lonely landscape still bears its ugly marks. In the adjoining towns of Camborne and Redruth where my ancestors once lived, the straight streets of houses run in the direction of the line of mineral veins. There you will find abandoned mine-workings and rows of bleak, grey, granite houses built for the miners. Wide areas of derelict land are now covered with yellow-flowering gorse and prickly blackberry bushes; and in the midst of it all are crumbling engine-houses and stamping mills, all roofless with vacant spaces for windows. Their brick chimney-stacks look like gaunt sentinels gazing out upon the desolate land.

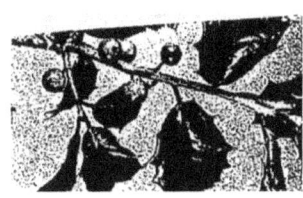

Holly

Samphire

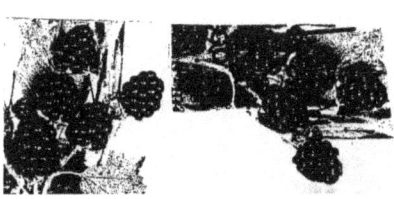

Blackberry

Engine-House

Mylor Creek – near Falmouth

Wild Ponies on Bodmin Moor

Treslothan – War Memorial and old Vicarage

SOCIAL CONDITIONS

189

A SON OF THE WESTCOUNTRY

It is more than one hundred years ago since a soldier by the strange name of Breaker Morant was put to death for breaking military rules.

Yet the life of this man continues to fascinate folks and a few years ago his life was the basis for a modem film which dramatically described events leading up to Breaker Morant's court-martial and execution. It gave viewers an accurate image of a skylarking, youthful and boisterous young man — and then concluded with the tragedy of his death by a firing-squad. He certainly had a strange nickname, but was his execution a miscarriage of justice and does he, perhaps, deserve a posthumous pardon?

We know that Morant went to Australia from England as a young exile in the 1880's at a time when the British believed Australia was a great destination for unsatisfactory folk — such as flawed, or less talented members, of the upper classes, especially for disgraced sons of the nobility.

Even the famous author, Charles Dickens (who had ten children) sent two of his sons to the 'Land Down Under' yet both died in debt. The writer, Anthony Trollope, sent a son (Frederick) in the same belief that Australia offered opportunities not to be found in England.

Breaker Morant was the son of Admiral Sir George Digby (of Devon) and intended for a naval career like his father, but he got into trouble (probably over an unpaid gambling debt) and was banished to Australia to seek his own fortune.

When Morant first arrived there he lived in the Outback

as a cattle-drover and horse-breaker, earning the reputation of "being the only Englishman ever seen here who could sit a buckjumper like an Aboriginal" and tales of his daring riding feats were told long after his death and became legendary throughout the land. There is no doubt he was well-educated for he loved writing bush-ballads and had them published in the Sydney newspaper under the pen-name of 'The Breaker'.

In 1899, at the beginning of the Great Boer War, he was working in Renmark where he joined the South Australian 2nd. Contingent and went to South Africa to fight against the troublesome Dutch. He was soon promoted to the rank of sergeant, and, after satisfactorily completing one year's service in the war, he was then invited to serve with the British Police Force in South Africa to help keep law and order against the Boer rebels.

At the end of 1900, like other Colonial soldiers, Morant was offered a commission in the Transvaal Constabulary, but refused because he wanted to go home to England and seek reconciliation with his family. Sadly, he seems to have been disappointed because he soon returned to South Africa and continued his career as a soldier in a special British corps named the Bushveldt Carbineers.

This corps contained both British and Colonial soldiers and had been formed especially to deal with ruthless Boer commandoes freely roaming a wild part of the country called the Spelonken. Perhaps, isolated from the rest of the army and therefore outside its jurisdiction, the corps may have shown a lack of restraint when dealing with the enemy; yet it is only fair to argue that the Boers showed little mercy to any captured Carbineers and had brutally murdered one of Morant's best friends.

Therefore the situation was inflamed and soon became

a matter of indiscriminate revenge on both sides, but it was only when Morant and four other officers put to death a Boer who claimed to be a German missionary, that they were put on trial and found guilty of twelve murders. Obviously, Britain did not wish to anger Germany.

The corps was disbanded and three of the accused officers (Handcock, Witton and Morant) were sentenced to death in February, 1902. The question that mystifies many folks is, "Why was Breaker Morant put to death if he had been such a good soldier against the enemy?"

In the British army "to be shot at dawn" was a punishment meted out to any soldier who disobeyed the rules and according to military records only four executions were carried out during the Great Boer War — although some years later, between 1914 and 1920, as many as 361 executions were carried out on soldiers as a punishment for desertion, cowardice, or sleeping on duty while serving in the First World War.

Such a stem measure shows how high was the standard of discipline in the British Army. Fortunately, the number of soldiers 'shot at dawn' declined rapidly by the end of the First World War, due to a greater understanding of a medical condition known as 'shell-shock' which occurs when a soldier is traumatized by combat.

Australia's request to the British Government to pardon Breaker Morant is rather strange since actually he was not a citizen of that country. Therefore the Australian Government did not have any authority to intervene, even if Morant was a volunteer soldier from there. Lieutenant Harry Morant received the same treatment as any other British soldier fighting against the Boers in that South African War (1899-1902).

There has always been a crusade and outrage against

Morant's punishment, but there really is no genuine excuse for his barbarous conduct as an army officer against prisoners in his care.

It seems that before his execution Morant asked a prison warden to take a message to his mother in England (and gave him an address). Some years later this man and his daughter visited a wealthy widow in Devon who was living in a grand house with servants. They were graciously received by this lady who was Morant's mother — and some years later the daughter described how that lady bitterly wept at such tragic news about the death of her son.

'the breaker' Poet Morant served in the Boer War but was executed by firing squad for murdering prisoners.

CORNISH POTATO CAKE

2 pounds (1 kilo) of potatoes. Set oven to 350F. or Mark 4. Boil and mash spuds and whilst they are still hot add the shredded suet (buy the real beef suet from butcher and shred it). Then add a teaspoon of salt, and enough flour to bind it all into a stiff paste (dough).

Press out with hands onto a greased flat tin, about 1 inch in thickness, mark into squares with a knife before placing it in the oven. Bake for about one hour, or until golden brown. Can be eaten plain or spread with butter

Cornish Heavy Cake
1 lb. flour
3 oz. sultanas
3 oz. currants
2 oz. lemon peel
½ lb. butter
½ lb. lard
Pinch of salt
Water to mix

Set oven to 350°F or Mark 4. Put the flour, salt and fruit into a mixing bowl and add the fat cut into small pieces. Mix to a manageable paste with cold water. Roll into an oblong on a floured board and put to cool for 10 minutes. Then roll out to about ¾ inch thickness, brush over with milk, put on a greased and floured tray and cook for about 45 minutes.

CORNISH POTATO CAKE

SURVIVAL AT SEA

By the middle of the nineteenth century the mines of Cornwall were producing three-quarters of all the copper in the world — as well as half the tin. Now, to extract all this ore my hard-working ancestors and their fellow-miners would have had to sink hundreds of miles of shafts and dig thousands of miles of underground tunnels.

Even if there were plenty of tin and copper beneath the ground, whole forests of trees would be needed to supply enough timber to make a sufficient number of pit-props and beams — and certainly there were not enough trees growing upon the face of Cornwall to be able to do this.

However, with the opening up of Canada's northern forests during the early 1800's, a flourishing international timber-trade was developed and soon Cornish cargo ships were sailing up the St. Lawrence River to Quebec — which possessed a harbour big enough to accommodate even the largest foreign vessels that came to buy Canada's wood.

Now it happened that in the year 1866 a Cornish barque named the *Jane Lowden* from Padstow (North Cornwall) set sail for Quebec to fetch a supply of timber. In charge of this sailing-ship was Captain Casey who had been hired by the rich mine owners and given sole responsibility to select the number of men that he would need for a crew.

There would be no danger as long as the weather was moderately decent because the *Jane Lowden* was a capable and sturdy sailing-ship. The voyage to Canada turned out to be quite pleasant and soon after arriving safely in Quebec harbour the barque was loaded with valuable logs of wood for her return journey.

The tall, rugged, granite cliffs that line the mouth of the St. Lawrence River have seen many shipwrecks over the years, so it was Captain Casey's intention to set sail for home ahead of the wild gales that blow in winter across the North Atlantic.

Therefore, by the 18th. December, the *Jane Lowden* and seven other freight ships were already loaded and eager to leave Quebec harbour. They sailed in steady formation down the St. Lawrence River until they reached the mouth of that great river.

THE 'JANE LOWDEN'
There were 57 shipwrecks off the Cornish coast during March in 1891

By the time the *Jane Lowden* emerged into the growling surf of the open sea, already ocean-breakers were surging angrily and the sea-spray slowly thickened into a dense fog. Above them the dark brown skies looked sullen and theatening, yet the tiny barque still sailed onwards to face the wild ocean. Strong winds began to blow and a violent hurricane struck without warning, causing the vessel to spin around upon the churning waves.

As fierce gales whipped up the sea into an angry roar, destruction seemed inevitable; and frightened mariners on board the *Jane Lowden* watched helplessly as the other cargo ships sailing ahead of them were hurled against the rocks and sucked down beneath the restless water.

With horror they watched the drowning bodies of men bobbing up and down like corks, their battered faces upturned to the black sky.

Heavy spray flew across the *Jane Lowden* in floods as her crew crawled about on deck trying to plug the leaks. Then her three gigantic masts snapped under the strain of the fierce wind in her topsails — and what with the roaring of the tempest and the violent rolling of the ship, Captain Casey and his crew were compelled to cling fast to the rigging.

Slanting sleet and hail descended upon the terrified mariners as they clung helplessly to the yard-arm. Soon the ship's rigging was coated with thin ice and the men's frozen fingers could scarcely hold the ropes.

They watched in disbelief as all the other timber ships completely disappeared under the phenomenal pressure of the wind and the pounding waves — with the loss of all lives.

Meanwhile the *Jane Lowden* tossed and pitched like a swirling piece of flotsam upon a gigantic mill-pond. Listing perilously, the crippled barque lay side-on to the pounding waves for thirty minutes before she finally turned over, thus throwing Captain Casey and his seventeen crewmen into the turbulent waters.

After many anxious moments eight of the crew were able to struggle back on board, but the other nine were lost at sea. Captain Casey took the helm himself and steered the *Jane Lowden* up and down the mountainous waves as if he were driving a train on the scenic railway.

The heavily-laden barque plunged and rammed her bows into the heavy surf with deafening thuds, rolling so wildly that her stern was often out of the water completely. Yet her brave captain still clung to the wheel, although cataracts of water deluged his ship and threatened to wash him overboard.

But it was useless. When the gale got worse, the eight surviving crewmen had to lash themselves to the mizzen mast. Then, after two hours when the hurricane had passed, they were able to climb higher up the rigging to keep dry.

Nothing happened until January 6th. when one of the crew, Alfred Bolton, fell from exhaustion onto the deck and at nine that evening he died. The next morning they committed his body to the deep.

The seven survivors had now been fourteen days without food or drink, but in spite of Captain Casey's wise advice to his desperate crewmen, they insisted on drinking the salty sea-water which eventually drove them mad with thirst.

On the 7th. January William Thomas died, but nobody had the strength to throw his body into the sea. The following day four more men died from exhaustion, cold and hunger — which left only Captain Casey and the ship's carpenter alive and still lashed to the rigging.

Then on the 10th. January the carpenter died, so now the

only survivor was the captain and by some miracle he was actually still alive ten days later when he was spotted by a passing barque, the *Ida Elizabeth* from Rotterdam.

Dutch sailors hastily untied him from the top mast and gently nursed him back to health, although he only weighed 48 pounds (24 kilograms) when rescued. Yet miraculously he survived and was strong enough to return to his wife and children in Padstow a few months later.

As improbable as his rescue may seem, no one denies that Captain Casey was a very lucky man to be found alive after such a terrible ordeal. Yet he never went to sea again — and who could blame him?

HE CONVERTED THE CORNISH MINERS
JOHN WESLEY (1703 – 1791)

"The best of all is, God is with us "—was his assurance.

- He began the Methodist Church which is now world wide.
- He was one of the first to hold Sunday Schools to teach girls and boys to read and write, and said : " You are in God's school, and He will teach you one lesson after another, till you have learned all His holy and acceptable will."
- He rode through the country on horseback to preach. In a single day he would ride seventy miles and preach three sermons.
- He roda more than 250,000 miles, and preached 45,000 sermons.

- In 1748 he founded a school for boys at Kingswood, Bristol, and wrote the text books.
- He published 233 original works on a variety of subjects.
- He compiled a Christian library. He wrote a four volume History of England.
- He wrote a book on Birds, Beasts and Insects.
- He wrote a medical book and sec up a free medical dispensary.
- He adapted an electrical machine for healing, and cured more than a thousand people.
- He set up Spinning and Knitting shops for the poor.
- He received £40,000 from his books, but gave it all away.
- He never wasted a piece of paper, a cup of water, or time.
- Historians write that John Wesley saved England morally and spiritually.
- He always listened to the kindly advice of his mother.
- He was especially fond of children and young people.
- He was always sweetly composed and sweetly disposed.

JOHN WESLEY

Poverty, violence and a contempt for the law were common amongst the hard-drinking, wild-living members of Cornwall's mining and fishing communities during the 18th. Century. The Church offered little personal contact because it was the territory of mine-owners and landed gentry who did not mix with the lower classes.

When the preacher, John Wesley, made the first of over 30 visits to Cornwall in 1743 he was met with suspicion and opposition. On several occasions his life was put in danger when he was pelted with stones and set upon by hounds. But Wesley persevered and made several visits until his courage was acknowledged and his simple message was accepted.

He travelled on horseback, visiting towns and villages from Launceston to St. Just and from Polperro to St. Ives — preaching first at small meetings in houses and cottages and then later at large open-air gatherings. His fiery preaching and the people's passionate singing converted many folks to Methodism and soon the miners were building small chapels along the country lanes.

For food and shelter Wesley relied on the kindness of villagers — and he often ate the blackberries and rosehips that grew in the hedgerows. Special accommodation was provided for him at Trewint (near Altamun) by the generous owner of a large house (which can be visited by people today). Sometimes, Wesley would ride 50 miles in three days.

Many of Wesley's best meetings were held at Gwennap Pit which was a disused mine pit that formed a hollow in the

John Wesley, founder of Methodism, who rode about the County for 50 years preaching the Gospel to poor miners, often in the open air and in all weathers.

ground and where people sat in a circle at various levels. The speaker could easily be heard when he stood at the bottom of the pit. Methodists still congregate here for their annual Whit Monday service. Nearby, a small memorial chapel tells the story of John Wesley's work in Cornwall.

JOHN WESLEY AND THE METHODISTS

The parish churches of Cornwall preserve the names of many early saints, but it is the many chapels built in country lanes and fields that serve to remind us of the heroic life of one man — John Wesley. With his brother, Charles, he first visited Cornwall in 1743. Their main object was to preach the Gospel of Christ to both high and low, but they experienced a great deal of opposition at first, even from the clergy who had grown rather slack in their duties.

The drunken miners were eventually converted and many of them even became lay-preachers. The miners built many little chapels in their spare time when they were not toiling down the mines. One of the best known preachers in the Camborne area was a poor miner by the name of Billy Bray.

The early Methodists were very strict in their ideas of right and wrong. That a woman should take pride in her clothes was thought of as sinful — as it was for a man to smoke. Billy Bray once said about the artificial flowers that women of the time used to wear on their hats, "I wouldn't mind you having a wagon-load of them on your heads, if they would do you any good, but it wouldn't. And everyone knows that flowers only grow in soft places."

Preaching another time against

tobacco, Billy quaintly remarked, "If the Lord intended man to smoke, He would certainly have made a little chimney at the back of the head for the smoke to pass through. But as He did not, I don't think He intended men to smoke."

Billy Bray must have made people laugh when he spoke like this, but his religion was a real one. It brought great happiness to him — and often before going underground at the beginning of a shift, Billy would kneel down amongst the other miners and pray, "Lord, if any of us must die today, let it be me. For they are not happy, but I am."

Though he was poor and his work hard, he once said, "I can't help praising the Lord. As I walk along the road I lift up one foot and it seems to say, 'Glory' and when I lift up the other foot it seems to say, 'Amen'. I can no more help praising God than the birds can help singing."

TREWINT

In Cornwall, the busy A30 road carries visitors from Launceston to Bodmin and beyond. Near Five Lanes is the hamlet of Trewint with a place all its own in the Wesley saga.

One summer day in 1743. Two of John Wesley's advance agents. John Nelson and John Downes. tired and hungry, asked for refreshment at a house with a stone porch the home of Dlgory Isbell a journeyman Stonemason. In his absence his wife, Elizabeth, entertained the two strangers who on leaving insisted on paying and then knelt and prayed — "Without a book/"

The house with the stone Porch

The Prophets Chamber

The story of these unusual visitors, with such unusual ways, was told to Digory on his return. A year later John Wesley himself, wet and weary, was entertained in the Stonemasons house and left a rich blessing behind. One evening Dlgory Isbell read in his Bible of the Shunamite woman who built a "Prophet's Chamber" for a man of God. "I will do that" said Digory and he did.

Trewint became a flourishing Methodist Society but when other chapels were opened the Trewint rooms fell into disuse and eventually became a roofless ruin.

In 1950 the Isbell house and the Wesley rooms were suitably restored. Services are now regularly held in the latter, believed to be the smallest Methodist preaching place in the world.

The A30 Road symbolises the stress and strain of modern life. Digory Isbells house at Trewint calls the soul to prayer and peace. For those who will linger and listen there, voices will speak of the riches of yesterday providing a thrill for to-day and a challenge for tomorrow.

The Prayer Room, used and loved by John Wesley.

Antique Collecting Box

To enter that tiny room fey a narrow, twisting staircase is to leave behind the stress and strain of modern life and hear once again Wesley's call to prayer and peace. Every visitor cannot help font feel Wesley's presence within those white-washed cob walls.

As you may know, John Wesley was the fifteenth of nineteen children and his father was the vicar of a Parish Church. At the age of six John was trapped in his nursery by a fire, but had the presence of mind to stand on a chest at the window where he was seen and rescued. His mother called him, "A brand plucked from the burning".

Here is the advice that Wesley gave to his followers and which is as applicable today as it was then: -

"Do all the good you can,
By all the means you can,
In all the places you can,
At all the times you can,
To all the people you can,
For as long as ever you can."

Digory Isbell"s Cottage, Trewint, Cornwall.
Where John Wesley preached and rested.

John Wesley preaching to Cornish "tinners" at Trewint.

He wrote in his journal that night, (15th July 1745), "I never remember so great an awakening...from Trewint quite to the seaside."

Cornwall during the latter part of the eighteenth century experienced a revival in religion and this was largely due to one man, JOHN WESLEY. With his brother, Charles, he visited Cornwall in 1743 and later, preaching in the open-air and converting the people. He would start the day at five in the morning and travel many miles to preach in four different places before sunset. They had little food and often ate only  the blackberries that grew wild along the hedgerows. Many little chapels began to spring up, built by miners or fishermen, with their own hands in the few short hours of leisure left them after work. Sadly, today, chapels like the one shown here, have been bought and converted into private houses because folks are returning to their irreligious ways and no longer attend Sunday services of worship.

MINERS or *FISHERMEN...*

ROUGH JUSTICE

Like other unemployed miners, one of my Moyle ancestors set sail from Falmouth (Cornwall) for North America in 1848. After arriving in California, he found the main form of transport was by steamship for there were no railroads in America at that time.

Great paddle-steamers carried passengers and cargo up and down the great rivers, so Moyle found it was the easiest and most popular way to travel. However, sometimes an alternative means of transport was by stage-coach, although the ride was always a bumpy one because of the very rough, stony roads.

After crossing over many mountains, Moyle eventually arrived at a lonely valley known as Deer Creek where he found several of his fellow Cornishmen hard at work digging for gold. Not wishing to poach upon their territory, Moyle suggested to another man that together they could search for gold in a higher part of the valley.

For many weeks, Moyle and his partner laboured from dawn to dusk (except on Sundays) and soon Moyle found enough gold nuggets to fill a leather bag which he hid behind a loose rock. One day he and his partner left their tent to dig a little further upstream and on the way they passed a swarthy-looking, black-bearded stranger.

After returning later that afternoon, Moyle went to check his bag of gold that he had carefully placed behind a large rock on the mountainside. It had vanished.

Immediately, Moyle and his partner scrambled down the ravine to where the other miners were working.

"Did you see a stranger come this way?" asked Moyle.

"Yes, he hurried past here a short time ago," they replied.

"He has stolen my bag of gold," explained Moyle, "and I need your help to catch him."

"We hate thieves," the miners replied. "Yes, we'll come with you to catch him. He can't have gone far on foot in this hot weather. We should catch him in Newtown."

The crowd of angry miners hurried down the mountainside and found the stranger in a saloon where he had just ordered a glass of beer to quench his thirst.

"You stole my gold!" yelled Moyle at the man. "Give it back!"

"Prove it," the stranger replied, in a cool, insolent manner. "Look in my pockets if yon want to."

"Search him!" the miners shouted; and before he could run away they fell upon him and tore off his coat and trousers. There beneath his shirt and tightly tied around his waist was the missing bag.

"Arrest him!" the crowd shouted; and soon his hands were tied behind his back with strong rope. The bag of gold was given to the landlord to hold until Moyle could prove it really was his stolen property.

Then a "Miners' Court" was formed (for there was no sheriff in Newtown back in those early days) and the miners soon elected a judge from amongst their number — as well as two of their more talented men to defend each side of the case.

In front of this hastily-convened court Moyle had to describe in great detail both the bag and its contents; which he did with such accuracy and sincerity that everyone present knew that he spoke the truth.

Moyle explained how the bag weighed so many ounces; how much the gold pieces individually weighed; and even described the various shapes of the nuggets.

When the bag was carefully examined, the contents were just as Moyle had described them. Thus, without any further delay, the prisoner was found "Guilty".

"String him up!" yelled some of the miners who wanted the culprit to be hanged from a tree. But others were against killing him because of the seriousness of sending the poor man into Eternity before he had time to prepare to meet his God.

Then the suggestion was made that he should be branded with a red-hot iron in the shape of a letter 'R' to signify he was a robber and the mark to be placed on one side of his face for all to see and be warned of his wicked ways.

As well as branding, the Judge declared that the thief should receive on his bare back two dozen lashes to be applied by the injured party — namely John Moyle.

So, a vote was taken by the entire company — and by a majority of only three there were more for branding and flogging than for hanging.

Then the iron was shaped into a letter 'R' and the thief was tied to a tree. However, when the iron was applied to his face it was too hot to make any readable letter and simply shrivelled all the skin down that side. Then he was stripped to his bare back and a rough whip was made for the flogging from several horse ropes plaited together.

He got it severely from John Moyle who was a very big, muscular man. His back was nothing but a mass of torn flesh

when he was eventually let loose. The thief departed with the words of the Judge still ringing in his ears — "If you are caught stealing again, you shall be hanged by the neck until you are dead."

Apparently, the severe punishment and the dire warning had no lasting effect upon this man for he continued robbing. He was finally arrested by the civil authorities and hanged in a Nevada jail.

THE CORNISH IN AUSTRALIA: A FATAL MISTAKE

From the beginning of Cornwall's history, the majority of Cornishmen have been tinners, or copperers, even though the work was always hard and dangerous.

However, by the 1860's the world's over-production of tin and copper resulted in the closure of many Cornish mines and so began a great exodus of miners to other countries where they could still earn a living. Overseas the money was good for a miner, although his wages still depended on sheer physical strength and manual dexterity.

In 1848 my grandmother's cousin, Thomas Vivian Moyle, left Camborne as a young man of twenty and emigrated to South Australia to seek his fortune. His father was a Mining Captain and so mining was in his blood, yet he decided to break away from family tradition; leave his mining job; and take a sailing ship to the opposite side of the world.

Thomas soon discovered that the young colony of South Australia was a land of boundless opportunity. Countless immigrants were arriving daily on her shores and he noticed there was an insatiable demand for accommodation and hospitality. In fact, Thomas Moyle saw a profitable future for himself as an hotelier.

In 1855 Thomas married a young widow (Elizabeth Crase) whose first husband had died on the Ballarat diggings; she had lost a baby there, too. So now, with a hard-working wife to help him, Thomas became a popular publican in country towns such as Hamilton, Kadina, Kapunda and Kanyaka.

Then in 1867 Thomas took his wife and daughter to Adelaide where he became owner of the "Strathmore Hotel" in North Terrace. Less than three years later he purchased the "Rising Sun Hotel" in Auburn and spent the following seven years there.

At fifty years of age he retired from the hospitality business and took his wife and daughter to live on his country estate, "Orange Grove". It was a very grand house with large gardens and quite convenient to Adelaide where he could visit his brother, Henry Vivian Moyle, a member of the South Australian Parliament.

After so much hard work "Down Under" it is sad to relate that Thomas did not enjoy his retirement for long, but met a sudden and tragic death on 24th. January, 1888. It happened long before the motorcar, in the days when people travelled by horse-drawn vehicles.

During the morning of that fateful day, Thomas drove his horse and trap into the city to meet a relation, William Claxton, with whom he had some business affairs to discuss.

The two men dined at the "Clarence Hotel" in King William Street and after lunch William Claxton bought Thomas a couple of drinks to celebrate their successful transaction.

Unfortunately, Thomas was suffering from an attack of dysentery, no doubt brought on by damp clothes for it had been raining heavily all morning. Visibility was poor when the two men bade each other farewell outside the hotel.

No doubt Thomas had only one thought in his mind — and that was to drive home and change into some dry garments. So he quickly climbed into the trap waiting beside the hotel.

By the time he realised that the vehicle he had entered did not belong to him it was too late. The high-speed quadruped raced away like a tornado as soon as Thomas picked up the reins.

Witnesses later described how they saw Mr. Moyle travelling at a furious pace along King William Street towards the River Torrens at about 1-30 p.m. and all agreed that the driver had obviously lost control of his horse.

Such was the animal's speed down the main street of Adelaide that when the horse attempted to take a corner the trap capsized and crashed with its spinning wheels uppermost. The shafts were broken as the horse turned a complete somersault, but then the fiery steed staggered to its feet and by means of the traces continued its mad race, dragging the overturned contraption even further.

In its headlong pursuit the horse forced one of the wheels over Thomas's body, thereby crushing both his legs. Fortunately, when Thomas was thrown out of the trap his neck was broken, so death would have been instantaneous.

At the Inquest, two days later, it was revealed that Thomas had taken somebody else's horse and trap which had been parked next to his outside the "Clarence Hotel". The Coroner said he could understand the mistake because both horses were about the same height and colour.

But Thomas's trap had two wheels while the other vehicle had four. No wonder, at this point in the proceedings, the Coroner began to think that Thomas Moyle was too drunk to count.

It was unfotunate, indeed, that the brown horse Thomas took in mistake for his own was a young, high-spirited, former racehorse; whereas Thomas's faithful steed was an elderly, quiet beast which always moved at a slow and steady stroll.

William Claxton testified on oath that his cousin was not drunk when they left the hotel, but was suffering from acute pains in the stomach brought on by a chill through wearing wet clothes. Also, William described how the heavy rain made visibility poor.

Thus, the Coroner was given a clearer picture of the sad circumstances leading to Thomas Moyle's tragic accident.

SOCIETY

It is interesting to note that wherever Cornishmen travelled throughout distant lands, they took the art of wrestling with them. In 1861 the wrestling champion of California was Thomas Eddy, of St. Austell, who won a prize of 275 dollars; whilst the second prize of 75 dollars was won by Thomas Mitchell, of Gwinear.

In olden days one of the chief occupations of Cornishmen was wrestling and it was a favourite pastime throughout England generally. (There is the famous match between Orlando and Charles in Shakespeare's play, 'As You Like It'.) At the battle of Agincourt (1415) a Cornish contingent marched onto the battlefield carrying a banner depicting two wrestlers 'in a hitch'. In 1662 a writer says, "The Cornish are masters of the art of wrestling"; but in Cornwall at least the sport was clean and manly, whilst the Devonshire style was very brutal because kicking was allowed and the wrestlers used to wear heavy iron-shod shoes so that by the end of the match their legs were streaming with blood.

The other chief Cornish sport in olden days was hurling, played between villages using a wooden ball covered with a casing of silver. The villagers (about 20 or 30 a side) would scramble or scratch for the ball and they used their church towers as the goals. It was a pitched battle and very rough so that at the end of the day the players would return home with bloody heads, broken bones and severe bruises. Hurling was played in other Celtic countries such as Ireland, Scotland, Wales and Brittany.

One tends to overlook the fact that after the mines closed there was also great unemployment among the hundreds of women who had worked all their lives as Bal Maidens, breaking and sorting out the ore above ground. Sadly, their attempts to find work as domestic servants in the rich houses usually failed because they were too uncouth.

The Cornish certainly believed in "witches and piskies' and their lives were ruled by ancient Celtic customs and traditions. Then, suddenly, in the year 1859 Cornwall became joined to the rest of England and found itself thrust into a 'modem and foreign' world. (That was also the year my grandfather, Richard Sampson, was born at Phillack.) The person responsible for this historic change was Isambard Kingdom Brunei (1806-1859) who designed and built a bridge to carry the railway into Cornwall. At a height of 100 feet the bridge spanned the River Tamar, joining Plymouth to Saltash. It became known as 'The Gateway to Cornwall', but was actually named after Queen Victoria's husband, Prince Albert. Of course, as soon as the railway reached Cornwall in the 1860's there came a new breed of traveller known as the 'holiday-maker' who certainly saved the economy after the mining era ended; but also began the destruction of all

<u>A STAGE COACH</u>
(These become redundant after the trains arrived)

things truly Cornish. In 1893 the first corridor train with 'steam-heated' warmth arrived and then travellers really appreciated the comfort and speed of this modern form of transport, now known as "the Golden Age of the Railway". Farmers were able to send their produce, such as fresh vegetables, up to the London mark changed the economy of Cornwall for ever.

Historians write about the Great Potato Famine in Ireland during the mid-eighteenth century, yet Cornwall also suffered from a potato disease in their crops about the same time and like the Irish this vegetable was their staple diet. So when the Cornish were asked to give money to help the Irish they replied, "What about us?"

The Cornish were the first to know about that great naval victory at Trafalgar and about the tragic death of Admiral Lord Nelson on the 21st. October, 1805. Such important news was carried to England by a Royal navy schooner 'H.M.S. Pickle' whose captain was a Devonshire man, Lt. Lapenotiere. In spite of a thousand miles of stormy sea the boat successfully reached Falmouth by the 4th. November; but then her young captain had to face a journey of 266 miles to London by post-chaise. As he raced through Cornwall he spread this news and so the Cornish knew before even the king and Parliament. With 19 horse-changes along the way, Lapenotiere reached Whitehall late on the 6th. November, announcing, *"Sir, we have won a great victory, hut we have lost Lord Nelson."* He then reported this news to the king who was so pleased with Lt. Lapenotiere that he gave him a present of a solid silver sugar-sifter from the royal breakfast table. When this naval hero retired he went to live in Cornwall (near Liskeard) and was buried at Menheniot. You can nowadays see his famous silver in the museum there.

H.M.S. "Pickle"

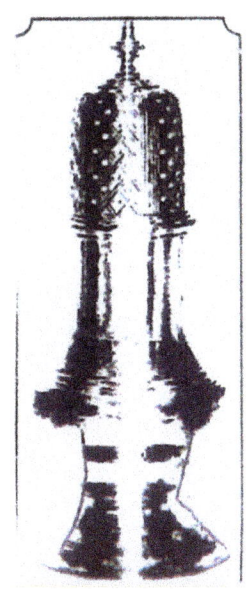

A silver sugar sifter

THE CORNISH KNEW ABOUT IT FIRST

In 1805, on the 21st. November, a great naval battle took place off the southern tip of Spain, at Cape Trafalgar, between British and Franco-Spanish fleets. That fierce naval battle raged for five hours, with twenty-seven British ships engaging the enemy's thirty-three, but it was this signal sent by Lord Nelson to his sailors which has become the famous motto for our fighting men in every war since — "ENGLAND EXPECTS THAT EVERY MAN WILL DO HIS DUTY".

One can scarcely imagine the noise of that great sea-battle caused by the splintering of timbers as wooden sailing-vessels smashed into each other and the sounds of shot and shell and screams of the dying upon the burning decks.

It was Nelson's flagship, "HMS Victory", that crashed into the French flagship, "Redoubtable", and all the time Admiral Horatio Nelson was on the quarter-deck in the thick of the action, leading his men by example as he always did, until he was struck down by a sniper's musket ball. They carried him below deck where he lay for three hours, dying from fatal injuries, surrounded by his loyal men.

It was only after he learnt that the British fleet had triumphed after a very long battle that Nelson uttered his final words, "KISS ME, HARDY. NOW I AM SATISFIED. THANK GOD I HAVE DONE MY DUTY."

It is the custom when sailors die at sea for their bodies to be committed to the deep — even the great Sir Francis Drake, who died from dysentery in 1596, was placed in a lead coffin and buried in the sea somewhere off the coast of Porto Rico. However, the body of Horatio Nelson, England's greatest naval hero, was preserved in a cask of brandy and carefully shipped back home to be given a State funeral and buried in St. Paul's Cathedral.

In those days news could be transmitted only by word of mouth, so a reliable naval officer was sent back to England bearing vital information about the important battle. His ship had to face a 1,000 mile journey and survive the fierce gales and storms of the Atlantic Ocean.

That messenger was Lieutenant John Lapenotiere, a 35-year-old Devonshire naval officer, and after fourteen days of battling wild hurricanes his ship safely reached the busy port of Falmouth, on the far westerly tip of Cornwall.

His crew stepped ashore to deliver the latest news — but the people's cheers soon turned to tears when they heard about the death of England's great hero. In Falmouth the church bells rang to celebrate a great victory, whilst the exhausted Lieutenant hired a post-chaise and drove quickly to London to tell King George III.

On his incredible journey through Cornwall, he stopped at Truro, Bodmin and Launceston to change horses — and in those places folks were told the story of Nelson's victory and death at Cape Trafalgar. Soon, every church in Cornwall was ringing its bells as the important news spread by word of mouth.

Lapenotiere deserves our praise because that weary sailor covered an astonishing journey of 270 miles to London in less than 36 hours by post-chaise and then delivered his message to the king in words which have become well-known throughout our English history: — "SIR, WE HAVE GAINED A GREAT VICTORY, BUT WE HAVE LOST LORD NELSON."

England was now safe from enemy invasion and Emperor Napoleon's ambition to conquer Britain was at an end. Britain ruled the waves and continued to do so for many years to come — as described in the words of two famous patriotic songs we used to sing, "Britons Never, Never, Never shall be Slaves" and "Land of Hope and Glory, Mother of the Free".

It was not until the late 1940's that Trafalgar Day was replaced with Armistice Day (11th. November) and parades took on a more sombre observance as people now remember the millions of men lost in two World Wars.

However, the Hero of Trafalgar will never be forgotten because his statue stands on a tall column, 170 feet high, in a London square. With a missing arm and eye (both lost in battles) our naval hero gazes down on a bustling city. At his feet lie four, huge, fearsome-looking lions carved out of stone which guard his monument — although throughout the years these lions did not prevent thousands of city-pigeons from perching on the famous man.

Monuments to Nelson's memory can be seen in many British towns and cities, but it is the famous 170 ft. column in Trafalgar Square that Hitler had his eyes upon during World War II. He knew that Nelson was a symbol of Britain's naval might and world domination, so with his planned invasion and a German victory over Britain, he was going to transport the lofty column back to Berlin. Hitler understood what it represented for England.

Two things that were not destroyed during the London blitz were St. Paul's Cathedral and Nelson's column. After the many bombing raids, St. Paul's stood alone on the top of Ludgate Hill while all the buildings around it had been wrecked. It seemed that Hitler could not destroy those two symbols of Britain's freedom.

The Battle of Trafalgar   *Admiral, Lord Nelson*

Visitors can now see a plaque on the quayside in Falmouth that describes the landing of Lt. John Lapenotiere with the important news of Nelson's victory. This was erected in 2005 to commemorate the bicentenary of the Battle of Trafalgar in 1805 and in Portsmouth you can see Nelson's famous flagship, HMS Victory, still in dry dock two hundred and ten years after her finest hour in the Battle of Trafalgar.

It may have happened a long time ago, but it is still relevant to Cornwall's character today.

SHIPWRECKED!

A brigantine was wrecked off Penzance, Cornwall, in 1888. Its crew of three men and a boy were saved by the courage of Cornish lifeguards whose lifeboat is seen here rowing ashore. People, gathered on the beach, watch this unfortunate ship in its hopeless struggle against raging surf and hidden rocks.

Cornish Tales

ALTERNON parish, (near Launceston) has a Celtic cross - and the church has one of the highest Towers in Cornwall.

St Nunn, the mother of St. David (of Wales) is buried here.

Jowle, the local town clerk in the time of Charles II who died at the age of 150 is buried here.

FISHING IN CORNWALL

With over 250 miles of coastline it is not surprising that fishing has been practised in Cornwall since Neolithic times. The most prosperous time of the industry was between the mid-18th. and mid-19th. centuries when every little harbour and cove had its own fishing fleet. The fish they caught provided cheap and wholesome food for the locals.

It is a fact that France, Italy and Spain lie opposite Cornwall across a narrow stretch of the English Channel, so Cornish fishermen found a ready market for their finny tribe in those three Catholic countries because fish was a necessary requirement for Lent and other religious fasting days.

Pilchards were the foundation of the industry because they arrived in huge shoals close to the shores and were trapped by seine nets strung between three or four boats. The catch was assisted by a man called a "huer" from the top of a cliff — thus, he had a clear view and could direct the fishermen in the right direction of a shoal with his cries of "Hevva" and the use of semaphore-like signals.

Pilchard catches were enormous and provided the Cornish folks with their daily food. It is recorded that in 1834, at St. Ives, 10,000 hogshead of pilchard (30 million fish) were landed in just one hour. In each harbour there would be at least one fish cellar (a large undercover courtyard) where the fish were salted, packed into barrels and pressed before being shipped overseas. The fish-oil by-product was used as lamp fuel — and rotten fish were spread on the fields as fertilizer, so nothing was wasted. But over the years there has been a decline of the pilchard shoals, due to over-fishing and climatic changes, and so the fishing industry in Cornwall has seen a slump. However, today Cornwall provides the market with mixed fish,

A grey seal

The Huer's Hut, Newquay.

There was a saying that without pilchards the Cornish would have starved. These fish were plentiful and cheap in season. Along the coast a Huer's hut would stand on the highest cliff and when shoals of fish arrived the Huer (lookout) would yell down to the fishing boats.

CORNISH MYTHS

Cornwall has many curious and strange myths which are similar to some of the stories from Ireland. Of course, both places had Celtic communities and had similar histories. For example, Cornwall's most famous myth is about the hideous dragon-like creature of Celtic lore which was slain by St. George, the patron saint of England.

Another curious legend is about a Beheading Game where the participants take it in turn to chop off each others' heads. It is not a true story because with mythical magic the heads rejoin the bodies on the following day.

Another legend tells of King Balor who was warned by the Druids that he would one day be killed by his own grandson. This clever king thought he could outwit the Druids — so to prevent the prophecy coming true he had his only child (an infant daughter) imprisoned in a high tower for the rest of her life. She was cared for by twelve ladies and consequently she grew up completely unaware of any sex but her own.

Dozmary Pool can be found in a very isolated valley on Bodmin Moor and has always been viewed as a mysterious place. One myth says this pool (believed to be bottomless) is inhabited by a Cornish god condemned to dwell there for his sins — and when he tries to escape from the magic waters he is forced back by supernatural hounds.

But many Cornish folks believe that Dozmary Pool is the home of King Arthur's magic sword, 'Excalibur'. It is where the 'Lady of the Lake' gave the young king a magic sword — and where when he was dying, he ordered his faithful knight to fling it back into that same pool.

Cornish gods

Legends about giants are famous in Cornwall — perhaps the idea began when the tall Celts arrived about 500 B.C. and the Bronze Age people were very short.

This is the Giant Cormoran who dropped a large granite block into the sea — which is now known as St. Michael's Mount.

Children"s games throughout the Centuries

1. Blind man's Buff
2. Hoops. (wood or iron)
3. Spinning the top
4. Leap-frog
5. oranges and lemons (ends with tug-of-war)
6. Hunt the slipper

THE ADVERB GAME

A person is chosen to be "it" and sent from the room. During his absence the other players choose an adverb. Upon his return he asks a question—any question—of each player in turn, and it shall be the duty of each player to answer the question in such a manner that he will be acting the adverb chosen. If the adverb was "joyfully," he will be joyful; if "crossly," he will be cross; if "ungrammatically," he will be ungrammatical; if "absurdly," he will be absurd. All sorts of amusing adverbs can be thought of. When the player who is "it" finally guesses an adverb, the last person to answer his question must become "it" in turn.

A DOG OF MANY PARTS

The player who begins this game says "I have an awkward little dog." The next player says, "He is a bold little dog," and the third player, knowing that his adjective must begin with C, says, "He is a cunning little dog." And so the sentence is passed on, each player contributing an adjective that begins with the letter of the alphabet following the letter used by the person just before him. Each player is allowed one minute to think of his adjective. If he fails, he must fall out of the game and sit on the floor until the game is finished. The player who stays on his chair longest is the winner.

A game of Conkers in the School yard

THE LAST HANGINGS IN ENGLAND
A BRUTAL MURDER

The following tragedy took place in a small Cornish village and for years afterwards local folks would only mention it in subdued tones because they were so ashamed that such a horrible crime should happen in their parish.

This is the sad story of Willy Rowe who was born in 1899 to a hardworking farmer and his wife. Willy's parents owned a small farm near the fishing harbour of Porthleven and when Willy was old enough he worked with his father and two older brothers on the family's property.

He helped to milk the cows and feed the pigs and poultry; and he did other chores such as ploughing and planting seeds in the Spring. Then at harvest-time he would work in the fields with his father and brothers to dig up the potatoes, turnips and broccoli which were then sent by train to the lucrative markets in London.

In 1917 when Willy was 18 years old, he was conscripted into the Duke of Cornwall's Regiment. The war in Europe thundered with unabated fury and such was the demand for men that youngsters of 18 were being called from their homes.

They were young men, still really boys, taken as cannon fodder to be thrown into the Devil's bath of blood. Sadly, like thousands of others, Willy was torn from the bosom of his loving family — and his peaceful life.

But after just one week in the army, somehow Willy managed to escape from a training camp on Salisbury Plain and journey back to Cornwall — to his home.

Unfortunately for Willy, someone in the village reported him to the authorities and soon military police arrived on the doorstep to arrest him as a deserter. They took Willy away and put him in a detention centre.

Onca again, Willy was clever enough to escape from the army and return home, but he was determined not to get caught a second time. The farm was very isolated — and somehow his family managed to hide Willy so successfully that nobody else knew he was there.

As a 'wanted man' he had to remain hidden at all times; in fact, for the next forty years Willy became the family's invisible son — dead to the rest of the world.

While his father and brothers worked on the land by day — when people were most likely to be visiting the farm — Willy did his share of work under cover of darkness during the lonely hours of the night.

When the family had to sell up after the father's death, Mrs. Rowe and her three sons moved to a smaller farm about six miles from the village of Constantine (near Falmouth). Willy travelled in the furniture-cart, hiding himself beneath old sacks so that nobody would see him.

Nothing much changed at their new place which was known as Nanjarrow Farm. Even after his younger brother left home to get married and his older brother died, Willy and his mother still continued to work the farm together, doing the usual day-night shift.

Their house had four large bedrooms with dark passages and an attic, so it was an ideal place for Willy to remain

Box of Matches

invisible especially as the farm-buildings were situated at the end of a long, narrow lane and over three miles from the nearest road.

It was not until Queen Elizabeth the Second came to the throne in 1953 that the British Government declared an amnesty for all deserters from both World Wars. At last, Willy was free to come out of hiding and join the human race again.

Unfortunately, his mother died soon after he was granted this freedom so poor Willy found himself completely alone in the world. He was not excited by his new-found liberty because after hiding from everybody for forty years he had no friends. Anyway, he decided that actually he preferred to be alone.

Although he could now openly tend his cattle and pigs without fear of detection, Willy rarely left the farm. Once a month he would leave the house to go shopping and visit the local market; and, inevitably, he soon became known throughout the parish as a rich recluse who hoarded all his money.

One day while Willy was away from the farm on one of his rare shopping expeditions, a burglar ransacked the place and Willy arrived home to find 200 pounds and his mother's jewellery missing. This invasion of his privacy and the theft of personal property was enough to send Willy over the edge and from that time onwards he trusted no-one.

He nailed heavy boards across every window, as well as the front door, so that the only means of entry to the house was through the back door. Willy no longer used his upstairs bedroom, sleeping instead on a chair in the kitchen with a loaded shotgun by his side.

There was no piped water and no electricity in the old house, so Willy used to wash himself in the animal-trough outside in the farmyard. He became known for his lack of personal cleanliness and the house was full of dirt and grime.

Local gossip had it that the old man was sitting on a hidden fortune and soon this kind of talk attracted the attention of dishonest men.

Sadly, in spite of all Willy's precautions, on the morning of the 14th. August, 1963, his battered, bloodstained body was found lying face down in the mud of his farmyard. Whoever had done this dastardly deed had thoroughly ransacked Willy's house and torn everything apart in a desperate search for hidden treasure.

Two detectives were sent from Scotland Yard to assist the Cornish police with this murder investigation; and when an autopsy revealed that Willy Rowe had been brutally battered and stabbed at the same time they knew they were looking for more than one killer.

The detectives began by interviewing any known burglars who worked in pairs; at the same time other policemen routinely questioned all residents in the district. One villager whom the police interviewed was Russell Pascoe, the son of Willy's nearest neighbour. He admitted to knowing the Rowe family and even told police he had worked as a labourer on Willy's farm for a short time.

At last, under pressure, Pascoe broke down and confessed to committing the house burglary two years previously, but he produced a cast-iron alibi for the night of Willy's murder on 14th. August. He said he had spent that particular night with his mate, Dennis Whitty, and their three girlfriends in a caravan at Truro.

Now one of the local policeman was very suspicious about

the boastful way in which Pascoe produced this apparently water-tight alibi, and he explained to the London detectives that married men in his village just did not go around bragging about sleeping with other women.

This same policeman also happened to know that Pascoe was married to a very decent girl, the daughter of a local church minister. Consequently, the two detectives decided to investigate Pascoe's movements more thoroughly and discovered that he had recently left his pregnant wife and now lived in a caravan on the outskirts of Truro with his mate, Whitty, and three girlfriends. It seems that Whitty slept with one girl while Pascoe shared his bed with the other two.

This information gave the police an important lead and consequently they took the three girls into custody for questioning. It was not long before the young women cracked under pressure and actually confessed about what really happened in their caravan on the night of Willy Rowe's murder.

After being assured by police that Pascoe and Whitty would not be able to harm them, one of the girls said, *"The two men borrowed our nylon stockings to use as face masks and then left Truro on Whitty's motorbike."*

Another girl said, *"Whitty showed us the blazer he had borrowed to disguise himself as an airman."*

And the third girl told detectives how Whitty had boasted about his cunning plan to pretend to be a crashed helicopter pilot from the RNAS at Culdrose and thus persuade Willy Rowe to open his door by asking to use a phone.

This vital piece of information from the girls gave detectives the clue as to how Willy was tricked into opening his door to strangers. Then the three girls decided to speak further about what happened when the two men returned in the early hours of the morning.

They said that Whitty was covered with blood and described how both men boasted about killing Willy Rowe — and threatened to kill them, too, if they told anyone about it.

The murder of Willy Rowe was brutal to say the least. He was beaten with an iron bar about the head and stabbed a number of times in the throat and chest.

The three girls described how Pascoe looked nervous, but Whitty was laughing and smiling.

"How much did they steal from Willy Rowe?" one of the detectives asked the girls.

"Just a few quid and some matches," the girls replied, *"and Pascoe was laughing because he thought it was a huge joke to kill the old chap just for a few quid and some matches."*

On the evidence of the three girls, police searched the caravan and identified a box of Willy Rowe's matches. They found a similar box in Whitty's coat at the Truro Gas-Works where he worked. Frogmen later recovered the murder weapons — an iron crowbar and a sheath knife — from a dam on Willy's farm.

When Pascoe and Whitty realised they could not escape the maximum punishment for their heinous crimes, each man gave a different account of what happened when Willy Rowe opened the door to them. Pascoe's story was that he had only tapped Rowe with a small iron bar to render him unconscious and it had been Whitty who went mad with the knife and stabbed Willy Rowe several times. Whereas, Whitty said it was Pascoe who went wild with the iron bar and kept thumping the old man until his head was smashed to pieces.

Their trial took place in Bodmin from the 29th. October to the 2nd. November, 1963, before Judge Thesiger. The jury did not take long to reach a unanimous verdict of 'Guilty' with the proviso that as both men had played an active part in the killing of Willy Rowe it was only fair that both should be sentenced to death.

Chief Justice Thesiger placed a black cap on his head to deliver the sentence — *"they shall be hanged by the neck until they are dead".* He added that because they had murdered together they should hang together.

Pascoe (aged 24) was hanged in Bristol prison, whilst Whitty (aged 22) was hanged at Winchester; and, although in different places, they were put to death at the same moment of the same day, 18th. December, 1963.

They were the last Cornishmen to be hanged for murder because Capital Punishment was abolished in Britain the following year in 1964. Undoubtedly, Pascoe and Whitty had been responsible for the most brutal killing ever committed in Cornwall; and not even the most ardent advocates for abolishing the Death Penalty made any protests about never seeing Pascoe and Whitty again.

Willy Rowe's life had been a strange one, but he never deserved to be murdered. In effect, one could say that Willy died twice. The first time was when he was hidden by his family for forty years after deserting from the army in the First World War — when he was assumed dead by the rest of the world.

Well, the two Scotland Yard detectives may have solved the murder case, but they were still left with the mystery of Willy's missing wealth. The brutal killers had not found it — and neither could they.

"Where can it possibly be hidden if it is not in the house?" they kept asking themselves. *"The dead man is laughing at everyone by taking his secret to the grave with him."*

Once again they searched the farmhouse from top to

bottom, but found nothing. However, when they were looking into boxes and cupboards they noticed an exercise book containing words written in a foreign language; so they took it back to London with them to show to language experts.

Eventually, the weird-looking words were recognised as a modern international language known as Esperanto. It seems that during his forty years of incarceration Willy had studied Esperanto and subsequently made secret notes concerning the whereabouts of his wealth.

When the strange writing had been deciphered it led police to hundreds of hiding places around the farm. Finally, from various holes in walls, hedges and fields they recovered thousands of pounds — it was Willy's hidden fortune.

It is hard to believe that in London, members of the Committee of 100 (that same group known as the 'Ban the Bomb' party) demonstrated outside the Home Office in a final bid to save Whitty and Pascoe from the hangman's noose.

They had collected more than 2,000 signatures on a petition asking the Home Secretary to advise the Queen to exercise her prerogative of mercy — but all their efforts came to nought as most of the general public agreed with the verdict of hanging after those two men were found "Guilty of brutally murdering Rowe in the course of theft".

Even harder to believe is the fact that Whitty's fiancée, Bridget Hamilton, visited him before he was hanged. Pascoe's wife, too, must have been a very forgiving woman because she visited her condemned husband the night before he died. Yet, remember how he had left his pregnant wife to live with Whitty and three girls in a Truro caravan?

Newlyn Harbour

Fishermen's Cottages

Old Inn - Padstow

THE CORNISH IN SOUTH AUSTRALIA

IN MEMORY OF THOMAS HENRY VIVIAN MOYLE
who was accidently drowned in the River Murray
– NOVEMBER 10, 1879 –

It is worth noting here that "being accidentally drowned" was not an uncommon accident in those days. In fact, it has been estimated that one person died from drowning every day in South Australia because very few English-born settlers could swim and therefore were unable to teach their children to swim, nor could they rescue a person who fell into a river or dam.

It is said that there were few South Australian pioneering families who did not count one of their relatives among these drowning victims.

John Moyle and his wife, Avis Stephens, had sixteen children altogether — which was a large number even in those days — but from the previous information one can see how Death cruelly intervened to cut down the number of their offspring and only eight of John Moyle's sixteen children actually survived.

When the railway line was extended from Kapunda to Morgan in 1878, John Moyle's brother (Henry V. Moyle) built the first hotel to be opened there, and then in 1880 passed it over to John.

At that time Morgan was one of the many very busy river ports along the Murray River, with its high wharves and customs houses necessary for dealing with the cross-border trade. The arrival of the railways in 1880 gave a special importance to Morgan as the town would in future be a link between the railways and the river trade; and John Moyle and his brother, Henry, realised the significance and the potential for a thriving hotel business in this bustling port, a gateway into N.S.W.

It seems that tragedy was ever-present in their lives because soon after the family arrived to enjoy a change of scenery by the river their first-born son was drowned in its waters. Did he fall off one of the busy wharves? Was he paddling on a hot day and fell into one of the hidden water holes? Or perhaps he fell out of a friend's boat?

DEATH BY DROWNING AT MORGAN

An inquest was held before Mr. G. Brunskill, J. P., on Wednesday, November 12, at the "Commercial Hotel", Morgan, on the body of THOMAS H. V. MOYLE, a lad of 17 years, the son of Mr. John Moyle of that place, who was drowned with a man named George Walker in a large lagoon near the North-West Bend Station, in the gale on Monday afternoon.

James Stuart, a fisherman who was giving evidence, said, "I recognise the body as that of Thomas H. V. Moyle. He and the man, Walker, came to my camp between one and two p.m. on Monday, and we went out on the river with the intention of having a day's sport. We all got into my boat and crossed the river, and went into the lagoon where we spent an hour or two shooting ducks.

A shower came on and we sheltered under a bush; and after it was over we thought of starting for home. All four, including John Miller who had also gone hunting with us, entered the boat and got half-way across the lagoon when heavy rain began to fall. I saw the wind was coming and pulled for the shore. But when we were only 150 yards from the shore, a fierce wind struck us.

I could not continue the course for shore, so put the boat's head into the wind and let her drift stern first. I cautioned the others not to move, but told Miller to get the pannikin and bail out any water she might ship.

She ran in same direction for another 400 or 500 yards, but I realised boat was sinking, so told all hands to jump out and keep hold of the boat while they were in the water. I leaped out myself, and when I rose to the surface they were all in the water. The boat then surfaced and we all got hold of her and clung to her for some time.

The deceased managed to climb on the bottom of the boat, which was upside down. I asked him to come to my side, and assisted him to do so, but found that Walker had grabbed hold of him from the other side of the boat. I told Miller to clear Walker and push the deceased over; but while we were attempting to do this a wave struck us, turning the boat half over and throwing us all off.

On coming to the surface, I found the boat had drifted some yards to the leeward. I swam to the boat, but could not see deceased, nor did I see him afterwards. I think it probable that deceased was struck by some portion of the boat. I saw Walker struggle for about five minutes, then sink.

After hanging to the boat with Miller, we drifted into shallower water and were able to push the boat ashore. I feel sure that Walker had hold of deceased when I saw Walker attempting to swim."

Foreman asked — "What are the dimensions of the boat?"

Stuart replied — "The dimensions of the boat are 16 feet by 3 feet beam, and 14 inches deep. I consider her fit in ordinary weather to carry four people."

A Juror asked — "The sudden squall struck us about 5-30 p.m. so what was the boat like then?"

Stuart replied — "When the boat had the four of us in her she had a freeboard of eight or nine inches."

John Miller, labourer, gave evidence on oath next: — "I was with Stuart, Walker and deceased last Monday. We crossed the river together. I got out and walked along the edge of the lagoon to ease the boat over the shallow water. After the first shower of rain we got into the boat to cross the river and come home.

But soon after leaving the shore it came on to rain, and a squall struck us, and we had to let the boat drift head to wind. Water began to come in, and she gradually settled down in the water. All jumped out, and deceased got on the bottom of the boat which had turned bottom upwards.

Stuart asked deceased to crawl to his side of the boat so as to balance her better, but Walker had hold of him. The boat then turned over again, and I never saw Walker or deceased afterwards.

Foreman asked — "Do you consider the boat safe under ordinary circumstances for four people?"

Miller replied — "I never saw such a squall on the river before in all my time here."

Policeman, Corporal Ewens, said on oath: — "On Monday evening I received information from the Bend Station that deceased and a man named Walker were drowned. Started early Tuesday morning to make a search with a number of volunteers, and continued doing so until 10 a.m. on Wednesday morning, and was present when the body of deceased was found, near where we had been searching.

Examined the body and found a key, a one-pound note, and a tobacco pouch containing tobacco. Noticed no marks of violence except those which I consider to be caused by shrimps. Have also noticed a very slight scratch on the head as if caused by one of the grappling irons."

Found drowned, yet on the river's placid breast
No hearing, sighing of remorse doth rest;
O flowing, sparkling waters, thou canst, thou dost not know
Of all the grief thou sendest betwixt thy ebb and flow.
Thou heedest not, that thou hast cast ashore
A fair young face whose lips shall smile no more;
And thou carest naught he was an only boy,
A father's pride, a mother's joy.

This beautiful and moving tribute describes the 16-year-old victim as an "only son", although at the time John Moyle and his wife, Avis, had several daughters. Their drowned son had been named after his grandparents, Thomas Moyle and Mary Vivian.

HARRY MOYLE (1871-1888)

A second death from sunstroke in this neighbourhood occurred on Sunday last. The weather on that day was very hot. In the morning Mr. J. W. Watts, butcher of Main Street, with several of his employees was watering stock in a paddock near Scotty's Grave. When they had finished their task they assembled at the house in the paddock prior to starting back home.

Amongst the party was a youth named Harry Moyle, 17 years old, the youngest son of Mr. Thomas Moyle of this town. He and two other lads mounted their horses and went out of the paddock first, followed by Mr. Watts, Thomas Moyle (Junior) and the others. It was noticed that the lads were in high spirits, including Harry Moyle, who prior to starting off had drunk rather largely of cold water.

The procession had not proceeded very far when Harry Moyle was compelled to get off his horse on account of feeling suddenly unwell. He lay down under the shade of a tree close by the roadside and told his companions to go back and tell his employer that he was too ill to ride any further.

When Mr. Watts and the others came upon the scene they found the poor young fellow in a dying condition. Water was fetched from a hole close by and his head bathed and a messenger was at once despatched for Dr. Hamilton. A few minutes later, however, the young lad died in the arms of his brother, Thomas Moyle, who was also employed by Mr. Watts.

The body was placed in a trap and the homeward journey continued. When nearing Kapunda they were met by Dr. Hamilton who, after inquiring into the case, certified that death resulted *from sunstroke and the affects of drinking cold water when the body was in a heated condition. No inquest was deemed necessary. The deceased lad was spoken of very highly by his employer and general sympathy is expressed for the bereaved parents.*

The funeral took place on the next day (Monday) and was very largely attended. The hearse was flanked on either side by six of his comrades, mounted and dressed in accordance with the custom of their trade, and each wore a hand of black crape on his arm. The pony which the deceased had been in the habit of riding was draped in black and led behind the hearse.

("Kapunda Herald", 11/1/1888)

Lift was very hard for these early settlers who left Cornwall for the mines of South Australia. From time immemorial Cornwall had produced miners and the export of tin had been the very life blood of the community. Then at the beginning of the 18th. Century the mining of copper as well became more appreciated.

By the middle of the 19th. Century there were about 340 tin and copper mines employing 50,000 people and Cornwall was producing three-quarters of the world's copper. Then the discovery of cheaper and larger supplies of tin and copper in other parts of the world led to the falls in price which then made thousands of people redundant.

Australia eventually displaced America as the favourite goal for British emigrants most of whom came looking for gold — and in 1852 as many as 85,000 left for these shores. In 1875 there were as many as 10,576 Cornish men and women who left for Australia.

These included many of my Moyle and Skewes ancestors and although they may have made their fortune here — they also experienced tragedies, too, as you have just read.

THE WORK OF A ROYAL MARINE IN W.W.1 AND HE WAS A CORNISHMAN

Now, in the year 2014, after one hundred years, we are still overwhelmed with horror at the unimaginable numbers of soldiers killed on the Somme battlefields — but let us not forget all the sailors who were also killed during those war years.

In 1904, my father who had lived in the little Cornish village of St. Gwinear, ran away to Plymouth to join the Royal Marines. He was only fourteen years old, so began his sea-going career as a bugle boy in the Naval Barracks.

By 1914 when the First World War began, he was at sea, serving on 'HMS Essex' in Admiral Sir Christopher Craddock's fleet whose job was to protect British trade routes along the southern coast of North America and the West Indies.

They were over 10,000 miles from England, when the sudden appearance of a German Squadron in the Pacific caught Admiral Craddock and his men by surprise. Under heavy fire, my father's battalion of Royal Marines quickly landed their guns at Vera Cruz to fight the enemy, but the Germans decided not to take up the fight.

Then, just seven days later on the 1st. November, those British ships were attacked off Coronel, on the coast of Chile. Admiral Von Spee's superior German Squadron was well-equipped and in the ensuing battle hundreds of my father's shipmates, including the popular and well-liked Admiral Sir Christopher Craddock, found death in the Pacific waters.

It was an humiliating defeat for our British men who

fought with valiant hearts, although their ships were outclassed, outspeeded and outgunned by the enemy's five modern cruisers. This 'Battle of Coronel' was proclaimed in Germany as a great victory and everyone boasted that their navy could defeat and destroy the British in any future sea-battles.

I wonder if my father's life was ever the same again after this cruel experience of war. Of course, a marine is really a "soldier on a ship" whose duty is to operate the guns and when necessary to fight on land.

That brave Cornishman, Harry Saunders, next served on the Australian Station where British ships were required to help escort the Anzacs on their way to training camps in Egypt. Later in May, 1915, he landed with a battalion of the Plymouth Royal Marines on the Turkish Pennsula as part of a British Naval Division sent to help the Anzacs in their attack on Krithia.

When those Royal Marines landed at Cape Helles, they were amazed to see Australian soldiers bathing in the sea whilst enemy shells exploded above them and shrapnel rained down upon them. While the Marines took shelter, those tall, brawny, sun-tanned Anzacs splashed each other in the sea — and although some were killed on the beach by bullets, nothing could stop their pleasure.

My father admired their lack of fear and later said that if ever he had to go "over the top" again he would like an Australian on his left and an Australian on his right — such was his admiration for their courage.

I remember a large picture of 'HMS Malaya' on the wall of our front room — for that was my father's ship in the Battle of Jutland. This famous sea battle took place on the 31 May, 1916, and is considered the greatest naval combat in history.

The first battle shots were fired when our advance ships led by Admiral Beatty met a German fleet off the Jutland coast and in the ensuing battle both sides received severe damage. My father was working on the guns of his ship, 'HMS Malaya', and that great battle stayed on his mind until his death — for with his last breath he was re-living it by shouting, "Pass up Cordite! Pass up Lyddite!"

He told my mother how the German ships eventually ran away and how they quickly threw their dead overboard to float on the water like so much flotsam. Whereas the British ships were ordered by Admiral Jellicoe to stop and give every dead hero a proper funeral service.

My father remembered that as each man was reverently slid overboard he seemed to stand to attention and salute his ship before sinking beneath the waves.

The German fleet never sailed forth again to face our ships and their sailors were kept in port which led to a mutiny and eventually the collapse of Germany. During the rest of the war my father crossed the Atlantic Ocean no less than fourteen times on Convoy Duties in 'HMS Cumberland' — thus helping to blockade German ports and consequently starve the enemy into submission. When Germany's great fleet of ships surrendered to the British at the end of the First World War (as part of the Armistice arrangements) my father was serving on board 'HMS Royal Oak' as a member of the Plymouth Royal Marine Light Infantry.

It was the 21st. November, 1918, and on every ship sailors were ordered to stand at their battle stations for no-one could believe that this great number of enemy ships would give in without a fight. My father and his fellow marines were lined up on deck with guns and bayonets ready for action.

Suddenly a drum began to beat on 'HMS Royal Oak' as

the enemy ships approached and it continued beating warning rolls — a naval custom that goes back for centuries. The drum continued its beating all the time our British Fleet was slowly closing around the German ships to form a square — until the enemy was hopelessly hemmed in.

When Admiral Grant inquired about the drum he was told there was no drummer on the ship and never had been. The ship was searched, yet every man was reported to be at his post. Both officers and men on 'HMS Royal Oak' were eventually convinced it must have been Drake's drum because in the British Navy there has always been a special belief amongst sailors that Drake's spirit would be present whenever England was in danger. My father used to say it was the audible manifestation of the spirit of England's greatest sea-captain protecting them.

But the fighting did not end for my father, that brave Cornishman, because after the war he was commissioned to 'HMS Cairo' with Admiral Barrett and on arrival in the British colony of Hong Kong, their ship was ordered to Vladivostock where martial law was declared — and to make matters worse their ship was iced in for several weeks until their food on board ran out and they were starving.

When his ship was able to leave Vladivostock it was immediately ordered to Hankow on the Yangste River where the Royal Marines were armed and expected to keep law and order. Later they were sent further along the Upper Yangtse River to keep guard over British possessions. As you can see,

Harry Saunders
Master–at–Arms

life in the Royal Marines was not meant to be easy — certainly not for that Cornishman anyway.

THE BATTLE OF JUTLAND – 31ST, MAY, 1916.

6,000 men of the Royal Navy died and three battle cruisers, three cruisers and seven destroyers were lost.
3,000 German casualties and the enemy lost one battleship, one cruiser, two destroyers and four light-cruisers.

FOOD FOR THE OLD CORNISH FOLKS

Cornish Pasty

INGREDIENTS
- A little flour, to dust
- 100 g (4 oz.) shortcrust pastry
- 50-75 g (2-3 oz.) turnip, sliced
- 25 g (1 oz.) onion, sliced
- Salt and freshly-ground black pepper, to taste
- 100 g (4 oz.) beef (skirt or chuck steak), cut into 1.5 cm (½ in) pieces
- 175 g (6 oz.) old potatoes, sliced
- Milk or egg wash

METHOD
1. Pre-heat oven to 425 deg. F., 220 deg. C., Gas Mark 7.
2. Flour work surface and roll out pastry into a circle 20.5 cm (8 in) across. Place an upturned plate over pastry and trim around to get a good shape.
3. Put most of the turnip and all of the onion across centre of round. Season to taste.
4. Put meat along the top and well into ends. Season with a little salt.
5. Top meat with most of the potato and remaining turnip. Season with a little salt then top with remaining potato. Do not season top layer: salt directly in contact with pastry can make it taste bitter.

6   With a little water, dampen one side of pastry. If you dampen all edges or use too much water you'll find edges will slide rather than seal.
7   Fold damp side of pastry to other side and press together firmly but gently, so that you have a seam either down the side or across the pastry — whichever you find easier.
8   Crimp by pinching pastry with left hand and folding over with right hand, forming rope like effect. Tuck in end to seal.
9   Make a small slit in top with a knife.
10 Brush pastry with milk or egg wash and put on a greased and floured baking tray.
11 Bake for 20 to 30 minutes. Check pastry (if brown, reduce temperature to 325 deg. F., 170 deg. C., Gas Mark 3). Bake for another 20 minutes. Turn off heat and leave in oven for another 15 minutes with oven door shut.
12 Remove from oven and leave to stand for 5 minutes. If eating picnic style, put on to a cake wire for 15 minutes before eating.

Makes 1 pasty.

Cook's Note:
Pasties retain their heat for a long time. So, if you want to eat them an hour or so later, wrap in a clean cloth straight from the oven. It's said that a pasty wrapped In Helston would still be "hot" when you reached Exeter!

The pastry is rolled out into the shape of a round plate and then folded so that the top half is resting over the rolling pin. In layers, place the <u>uncooked</u> and thinly <u>sliced</u> turnip, potatoes and meat. Some modern recipes also say onions, but never use carrots, or any other vegetable; and never mince or chop these ingredients. Add salt and pepper as you wish, but never put salt on top layer next to the pastry. Now, double over the pastry and wet one edge before crimping the two edges together — not too wet or the edges will just slide. Then bake in hot oven as directed. (My mother used to bake a pasty for me and carry it on her bicycle to the village school at dinner-time. Wrapped in a cloth when straight from the oven a pasty will keep hot for a long time. It should only be eaten held in the hands.)

Starry Gazy Pie
INGREDIENTS
- 225 g (8 oz.) flaky or shortcrust pastry
- Egg wash

To Make Filling:
- 6 tbs. white breadcrumbs
- 150 ml (5fl. oz.) milk
- 2 tbs. chopped fresh dill
- 45 ml (3 tbs.) lemon juice
- *1 onion, chopped*
- 6 to 8 pilchards, cleaned with heads left on
- 2 hard-boiled eggs, chopped
- 150 ml (5 fl. oz.) scrumpy
- Salt and freshly-ground black pepper, to taste

METHOD
1. Pre-heat oven to 425 deg. F., 220 deg. C., Gas Mark 7.
2. Soak breadcrumbs in milk and once swollen stir in dill, lemon juice and onion. Mix well.
3. Into a piedish put fish with the heads resting on rim. Press stuffing over the top of fish and scatter over eggs. Pour over scrumpy and season.

4   Roll out pastry to cover piedish and press on firmly leaving pilchard heads exposed. Brush pastry with egg wash.
5   Bake for 15 minutes, then reduce temperature to 375 deg. F., 190 deg. C., Gas Mark 5, and cook for a further 25 minutes until pastry is golden brown.

Serves 4 to 6.

A CORNISH SPECIAL

INGREDIENTS
- 450 g (1 lb.) potatoes, cubed
- Salt and freshly-ground black pepper, to taste
- 450 g (1 lb.) cauliflower, broken into florets
- 50 g (2 oz.) margarine
- 175 g (6 oz.) back bacon, cut into strips
- 50 g (2 oz.) plain flour
- 300 ml (10 fl. oz.) milk
- 125 g (4 oz.) Cheddar cheese, grated

METHOD
1. Put potatoes into a large saucepan of salted water and bring to the boil. Cover and simmer for 10 minutes.
2. Add cauliflower to saucepan and bring back to the boil. Simmer for a further 10 minutes then drain, reserving 150 ml (5 fl. oz.) of the cooking liquor.
3. Pre-heat oven to 400 deg. F., 200 deg. C., Gas Mark 6.
4. Melt fat and fry bacon until crisp.
5. Stir in flour, then gradually add the milk and cooking liquor. Stir continuously until mixture comes to the boil.
6. Remove from heat, beat-in half the cheese and season to taste.
7. Gently fold vegetables into sauce then turn into a shallow casserole dish. Sprinkle with remaining cheese.
8. Bake, uncovered, for 15 to 20 minutes until cheese is golden brown. Serve hot.

Serves 4.

GINGER FAIRINGS

These biscuits were sold at Cornish fairs over the centuries and I often saw them being baked in the Cornish range by my father's elderly cousin, or her domestic servant. No recipe was required as these biscuits had been made in Cornish families for many generations.

INGREDIENTS
4oz. flour
2oz. margarine, or butter
2oz. brown sugar
grated lemon peel (opt)
1 teaspoon cinnamon
1 teaspoon ground ginger
1 teaspoon mixed spice
1 teaspoon baking powder
1 teaspoon bicarb. of soda
2 tablespoons golden syrup

METHOD
1. Set oven to 350 F or Mark 4.
2. Grease baking sheet.
3. Sieve dry ingredients together.
4. Rub in the fat with fingers.
5. Add the warmed syrup.
6. Combine to a smooth paste.
7. Roll mix into small balls.
8. Place on baking sheet.
9. Cook for about 15 minutes.
10. Reduce temperature to 325 F. or Mark 3 and finish cooking for 5-10 minutes so that the biscuits sink and crack into a familiar form.

POTATO OMELETTE

INGREDIENTS

3 eggs
½ lb. potatoes, boiled
1 oz. butter
some chopped parsley
salt and pepper

METHOD

1. Beat eggs and stir in parsley.
2. Cut up potatoes and add to eggs.
3. Melt butter in fry pan.
4. Pour in the omelette mixture.
5. Cook until golden brown.

*Stoke Climsland Church
where William Sampson, killed in a mine accident, was buried.*

CORNISH STEW

This is a Cornishman's traditional dinner and one that I never tired of when made by my mother, or elderly cousins. Potatoes and turnips grow easily in the mineral soil of Cornwall and these two vegetables were the basic food of working-class folks who could afford little else. Stew originates from the days of the old-fashioned kitchens where the peat/wood fires were kept burning all day and where it was a tradition never to let them go out. Of course, Cornish housewives of yesteryear never had to read a recipe — they were practical people and I just cannot remember ever seeing a recipe book inside a Cornish cottage when I was young.

INGREDIENTS
cubed stewing steak, but brown the meat first in a little oil in the pot. Add a pint of cold water to the meat, as well as the sliced potatoes, sliced turnips, sliced carrots and onions. Add seasoning and herbs, such as parsley. Combine all these ingredients in the pot and stir gently till almost boiling. Simmer for about two hours. Remember, *"A stew boiled, is a stew spoiled!"* Nowadays, this meal is cooked in a casserole in a slow oven.

SEEDY CAKE My elderly cousins loved "Seedy cake". Personally, I could not bear the taste (or smell) of caraway seeds, but I often watched the old folks enjoying this cake. Just beat 4oz. butter and 4oz. sugar together; add two eggs one at a time; sift in 4oz. flour with ½ teaspoon of baking powder and then 2 heaped teaspoons of caraway seeds. Use enough milk to produce a soft, dropping consistency. Bake in greased tin at 180C for just an hour.

"Cornish Riviera" Express Train from Paddington to Penzance and return

Soul cakes

On All Souls' Day, 2nd November, children would go a-souling, singing in return for cakes which they would take home to the family for Souls' Night dinner. They came in many different versions, such as this recipe from Shropshire.

Ingredients:
- 6 oz/175g softened butter
- 6 oz/175g caster sugar
- 3 egg yolks
- 1 lb/450g plain flour
- pinch of salt
- 1 tsp of ground mixed spice or allspice
- 3 oz/85g currants
- a little warm milk

1. Heat the oven to 180 °C/350 °F Cream the butter and sugar together in a bowl until fluffy, then beat in the egg yolks. Sift together the flour, salt and spice and fold into the egg mixture with the currants, adding

All Souls marks the beginning of winter, when the dead are remembered and the Wild Hunt rides

sufficient milk to form a soft dough. If desired a few threads of saffron can be soaked in the warm milk, straining it before use.
2. Divide into pieces and form into 24 flat cakes, marking each with a cross. Place on a greased baking sheet and bake for 10-15 minutes or until golden.
3. Children went soul-caking, singing: "A soul-cake, a soul-cake, please, good missus, a soul-cake. One for Peter, one for Paul, three for Him who saved us all". Soul cakes are often marked with a cross, in reflection of their religious origins — although they should not be confused with the Easter tradition of hot cross buns.

The children would also bake and take soul cakes with them, exchanging them for sweets and pennies, while the needy went door to door to be given cakes and alms. At Soul Night supper the cakes would be served, with extra portions laid out for deceased relatives.

In Britain, All Souls is also known to be the night of the Wild Hunt. This myth, widespread across northern Europe, tells of a spectral host led by the god of hunting, which charges through the night, striking fear into the hearts of all who hear it, and bringing tragedy to any who cross its path.

St. Michael's Mount

CAPTAIN PHILIP GIDLEY KING

King was born at Launceston, Cornwall, on April 23rd. 1758, the son of Philip King, a prosperous draper. He always wanted a sea-faring life and thus began his naval career at the age of 12 as a captain's servant in the frigate 'Swallow'.

He then served for five years in the East Indies and was promoted lieutenant to 'HMS Renown'. Four years later he joined Captain Phillip's ship and thus began their association which led to King joining Captain Phillip on Norfolk Island and later he was put in charge of that prison colony.

LAUNCESTON

It was in this small but ancient town in North Cornwall that Phillip Gidley King was born. He was the Governor of New South Wales (Australia) 1800-1806.

A CORNISH TRAGEDY

Newspapers always seem to contain stories about the worst side of human nature and in 192! the *Cornish Guardian* printed the case of Edward Ernest Black who was accused of murdering his wife. This newspaper states that Mrs. Black died from arsenic poisoning and soon afterwards her husband ran away.

Cornish police eventually found the fugitive in Liverpool (where he had tried to commit suicide by cutting his throat) and brought their prisoner back to St. Austell to stand trial. The *Cornish Guardian* described the accused man in great detail with these words: -

"When Black, a former insurance man and member of the parish church choir, limped into court he had to be assisted into the dock; and it was noticeable that he had now lost the air of self-confidence that had characterised his appearance on the first day of his trial His smart grey suit now hung carelessly upon him, yet there was an air of bravado about his smart blue and gold striped shirt and black tie — but the white linen collar failed to hide a very ugly, long gash upon his throat. There was a certain wildness about his face and a pallor about his cheeks which were accentuated by the blackness of his heavy brows and drooping moustache. His eyes were fixed intently throughout the proceedings on the face of each person who stood in the dock and upon whose evidence depended his life. Sometimes his head fell forward upon his hands, whilst at other times he nervously clasped and unclasped his hands continually. Occasionally, he would glance at his step-daughter sitting in the front row of the audience.

The facts that emerged from his trial revealed that Black was heavily in debt and that his wife, an invalid, was eighteen years his senior. Also, a post-mortem revealed that Mrs. Black had definitely died from arsenic poisoning.

When it was suggested that she could have poisoned herself, the Judge said that no one who had the slightest acquaintance with arsenic would desire death by that means because it was a most terrible kind of death by slow burning of the intestines. The Judge added that suicides generally used a quick poison and he had never heard of a case of suicide by arsenic poisoning.

It seems that Black made one major mistake in trying to cover up his crime because he swore on oath in the witness-box that he had never bought any arsenic from the St. Austell chemist (a branch of Timothy White); and when he was shown his signature inside the pages of the poison book, he insisted it was a forgery. The judge and jury were not impressed by his weak excuse. It took only forty-five minutes for the jury to return a verdict of "Guilty" and Black showed no signs of emotion when the Judge placed the black cap on his head to pass sentence of death with these solemn words: -

"You will be taken from this place to a lawful prison and from thence hence to a place of execution and there hanged by the neck

A judicial procession crossing the town square to the local court.

until you are dead and be buried within the precincts of that prison. May the Lord have mercy on your soul."

N.B. By the end of the 19th. Century, executions were no longer carried out at Bodmin prison in Cornwall, so condemned murderers were taken by train to Exeter Gaol, in the neighbouring county of Devon.

A CRIME OF PASSION

In 1925, two corpses were found lying on a classroom floor in the council school at St. Stephens village. The woman had been cleaning the room when attacked from behind by her former sweetheart. He slit her throat and then turned the knife on himself.

This double tragedy was a shocking event for that tiny Cornish village, especially as in such country places everybody knows everybody else. The dead man, Herbert Sandercock, was a labourer in the local china-clay pits and came from Bugle. His hapless victim was a pretty young woman named Sidonia Taylor who had lived in St. Stephens all her life and recently broken off her engagement to him.

She told her mother she wished she had never met him because he, frightened her. She told her friends that the engagement was a big mistake. Moreover, when Sidonia returned his ring he became quite violent and threatened to kill her. In fact, Sandercock was so jealous that he swore he would kill any man whom she dated.

He certainly had a strange way of showing his love because when they were engaged he often secretly followed Sidonia into St. Austell when she went shopping there — and he would spy on her every movement. She could tell he was following her because she saw his reflection in every shop window; yet when she challenged him about it he would say it was all in her imagination.

Once he took Sidonia to Plymouth and deliberately left her alone in the city centre. She was terrified, standing in those busy streets, surrounded by strangers and without any money — but her sweetheart seemed to enjoy playing such nasty tricks on her. Naturally, this innocent young woman was afraid when taken out of her familiar environment and eventually she became scared of going out with him. What was the reason for his strange behaviour?

After Sidonia returned his engagement ring and presents, she stayed at home every evening because she was afraid to go out for fear of what he might do to her. He had said that if he saw anyone else going out with her he would stab that person, but her parents advised her not to worry about Sandercock's threats and said he would soon weary of it.

But Sidonia became more and more afraid to go out to any social events in the village for fear of meeting her former sweetheart. The only time she left home was to carry out her duties as a school cleaner.

As for that jealous and possessive Herbert Sandercock, his last hours read like a Victorian melodrama. He had returned to his lodgings about mid-day and only partially ate his dinner; and when his landlady remarked upon his poor appetite he told her he was very upset by what he had heard at work that morning.

It seems that another labourer in the china clay pits had told several of his workmates that he was going to ask the good-looking Sidonia Taylor to be his sweetheart. This remark must have upset Herbert so much that not only did he lose his appetite but he also wrote letters to his father and brother.

He then packed a suitcase with all the new clothes he had recently bought from the village shop and returned them that afternoon. He then paid a bill at the shoemaker's shop before visiting the local barber to ask about the man who was going out with Miss Taylor — but the barber could not, or would not, tell him what he wanted to know.

This may have aroused Sandercock's jealous rage to the point of no return. Immediately, he crossed the road and quietly climbed through a window at the back of the school building, catching his former sweetheart unawares as she brushed a classroom floor.

One can only imagine Sidonia's fear as she glanced up and saw Sandercock approaching her with a knife in his hand. Her screams attracted the attention of nearby residents, but by the time help arrived it was too late.

AUSTRALIA'S FIRST FREE FARMER WAS A CORNISHMAN

James Ruse was born in 1760 in Launceston, Cornwall, and as a young man he worked as an agricultural labourer. His wages would have been a pittance and for some reason in 1782 he was desperate enough to steal some food — but he was caught and subsequently convicted at the Bodmin Assizes.

He was sentenced to seven years' transportation, so whatever he stole must have been worth less than 39 shillings otherwise he would have been sent to the gallows.

At that time Britain did not know what to do with its many prisoners because the victory of American colonists had closed that place to British convicts and, consequently, thousands of condemned creatures were crammed into prison hulks anchored on the Thames, or other rivers.

Cornishman, James Ruse, spent the first five years of his sentence on the prison hulk 'Dunkirk' which was moored in Portsmouth harbour. Eventually, 'Dunkirk' was sent out to Australia with the First Fleet and by the time it arrived in Britain's new penal colony, Ruse's term of imprisonment had almost expired.

The first Governor of New South Wales was Arthur Phillip, (1787 — 1792) a wise and visionary man, who was inspired by the idea of turning 'emancipists' (i.e. convicts who have served their sentence) into sturdy, hard-working yeomen. Therefore, he established a government farm to raise food and thus help convicts to become self-sufficient.

In 1789, Cornishman James Ruse was the first emancipist

chosen by Governor Arthur Phillip to be given an acre of cleared land and also a patch of raw bush at Parramatta. Phillip had noticed that this ex-convict was a hard worker — and possibly selected James knowing that he had grown up working on the land all his life and was 'bred a husbandman'. As well as the land, Ruse was provided with the necessary tools, some seed grain, and a small number of livestock.

As Governor Arthur Phillip had hoped, after just two years Ruse was able to support himself (and a wife and child) without the need for public charity. His reward was another 30 acres — the first land grant ever made in Australia — and by 1819, Ruse had increased the size of his farm to 200 acres.

The following description by James Ruse about his work was written down by a friendly officer of the Marine Corps: -

Ruse said, "I have now grown an acre-and-a-half in bearded wheat, half-an-acre in maize and a small kitchen garden ... My land I prepared thus. Having burnt the fallen timber on the ground, I dug in the ashes and then hoed it up. I worked only a small amount of land each day, by which means it was not like the government farms, just scratched over, but properly done. Then I dug in the grass and weeds. This I think almost equal to ploughing ... And just before I sowed my seed turned it all up afresh. When I shall have reaped my crop, I proposed to hoe it again, and harrow it fine, and then sow it with turnip seed, which will mellow and prepare it for next year."

Later, Governor Phillip gave land to other emancipists because he hoped that in this way the colony would become self-supporting.

Unfortunately, one of Australia's perennial problems is either too much water, or too little, and when the Hawkesbury

River north of Sydney flooded four times in the early 1800's, it washed away the crops of James Ruse, bringing him and everyone else to the brink of starvation.

Thus, having his own land did not end happily for James Ruse because he eventually lost it all through drought, poor harvests and labour problems. Drinking rum, or rather too much of it, was another cause of his downfall — and, sadly, he ended his days working as a labourer for another farmer.

He died in 1837 and the strangely-spelt epitaph headstone gives us an interesting description of his life: -

My Mother Reread me Tenderley
With Me She Took Much Paines
And when I arrived in This Coelney
I sowd the Forst Grain and Now
With My Hevenly Father I hope
For Ever to Remain

Cornishman James Ruse was Australia's first true pioneer because he was the first free convict to become a farmer 'Down Under'.

Convicts of the First Fleet

THE BRAVEST CONVICT WAS A CORNISHWOMAN

Lack of money is the root of all evil and it is true that poverty can drive people to desperate and sometimes dastardly deeds. Mary Broad was a Cornish woman from Fowey and when she was only 21 years of age she stole a cloak to keep herself warm.

However, when the shopkeeper chased her along the street in an attempt to recover his property, Mary resisted and the struggle ended in a violent fight for possession of the garment.

Thus, at the Bodmin Assizes on March 20th. in 1786, Mary was convicted of theft of a cloak and street robbery with violence and, consequently, she was sentenced to death.

Luckily, her sentence was commuted to transportation beyond the seas for seven years, so Mary found herself, with many others, bound for Botany Bay on a transport ship, 'Charlotte', as part of the First Fleet which sailed on May 13th. 1787.

En route to New South Wales while the ship tossed upon stormy seas, Mary gave birth to a daughter whom she named 'Charlotte' (for obvious reasons). But the question must surely be, "Who was the father?" because Mary had been incarcerated on a prison hulk since her arrest in March, 1786.

One of the male convicts on the 'Charlotte' was William Bryant, a Cornish fisherman, about 27 years of age, who in March, 1784, had been convicted of smuggling and 'for resisting arrest by the revenue officers who had attempted to seize illicit goods he had hidden in his house'. In those days, smuggling was very common along the rocky Cornish coast where French and Spanish ships could easily land their wine to avoid paying taxes.

It was during the long voyage that William noticed Mary Broad — the pretty young woman with a baby — so decided to help her as much as he could. They fell in love and no doubt formed a close bond as both were from Cornwall. Only four days after the landing of the First Fleet at Sydney Cove, on February 10th. 1788, Mary Broad married William Bryant.

Not long afterwards, a Marine officer was looking for someone reliable to put in charge of fishing boats moored in the harbour. When he heard that Bryant had been a fisherman from boyhood, this officer decided Bryant would be a suitable man for the job. Of course, the Marine officer checked that William had conducted himself commendably during the long voyage.

Sea-food would be a cheap and easy source of food for the new settlers at Botany Bay, so Bryant was made responsible for the daily catch which was in demand by everyone.

However, he could not resist the temptation to make a little easy money, and secretly sold some of the fish privately. He escaped detection for twelve months until someone reported him to the authorities. Bryant was found guilty of stealing public property and given 100 lashes, but he was retained in his job as a fisherman although at a lower rank.

In 1789 a lack of rain had destroyed their crops so the summer harvest had yielded only enough grain for three weeks' supply of bread; and by January, 1790, the colony's food was at a dangerously low level because the food left in store had been eaten by the rats and the natives had killed the few cattle.

There was gloom and sadness throughout the place because many starving convicts began to die and others were too weak to work. Sadly, there was no help for them from the mother country who appeared to have forgotten these occupants of her distant colony.

Even people invited to dine at Governor Phillip's house were asked to take their own bread to put on the table. Slowly the shadow of starvation and famine fell upon this isolated settlement until there was only one way to stay alive — escape!

Perhaps escaping was a dangerous remedy for starvation because the risks were very high. Some convicts tried to walk overland to China (a country which they thought was joined to the Australian continent) but they died of exhaustion, thirst and hunger, or were killed by natives.

Other convicts attempted to escape by sea in stolen boats, but were never heard of again because they drowned in the mighty ocean.

During this terrible time of food shortages, Mary's second child was born She named him Emanuel (a gift from God), but now her situation looked very bleak with two children to feed. Thus, after much persuasion, she agreed too her husband's proposal that she, her young children, and seven of his convict friends should escape from the starving colony.

It was a desperate solution — however, at the time everyone had heard about the mutiny on the 'Bounty' and how William Bligh had successfully rowed across the Pacific Ocean. Thus, inspired by Bligh's achievements, Bryant and his convict friends carried out a desperate plan to reach Timor by stealing the governor's cutter — a six-oared boat in mint condition.

However, they needed to carry enough provisions for the survival of nine adults and two children on that long journey of 3.254 miles; so during the next few days Bryant and his mates stealthily gathered provisions for the journey and cautiously concealed foodstuffs in the cutter. That clever Cornishman had also secured a map of their intended route, as well as a quadrant, two muskets and some ammunition.

They packed flour, rice, pork and about 10 gallons of water — as well as cooking utensils, bedding, two tents, tools, fishing lines and hooks. When all was ready for their long and dangerous journey, they chose a night when there would be no ships in the harbor and no moon in the sky.

It was 10 p.m. on March 28th. 1791, and pitch-dark when their stolen cutter slipped past the Marine on lookout duty at South Head — and thus began their escape across the Pacific Ocean and back to Britain. How they had managed to steal the cutter and load her in the dark with all their gear and get everyone on board without detection, was undoubtedly a miracle.

Then began a bid for freedom that would take those wretched escapees half-way across the world. Their journey up the Australian coast was dangerous, especially whenever they tried to land for they were continuously at the mercy of wild, savage natives.

But they must have fresh water, so often they had to risk the dangerous process of beaching and launching their boat. Frequent gales caused waves as high as mountains and the crew had to constantly bail out water to keep the boat afloat. Every moment they expected to sink to the bottom of that angry ocean.

The Great Barrier Reef gave them some protection, but near the shore they were pursued by several fierce natives in war canoes. Luckily, they outdistanced them and safely landed on the coast of Arnhem Land before crossing the Arafura Sea where they sailed along the coast of Timor, ending up in the Dutch territory of Coupang.

The Dutch Governor accepted Bryant's story (that they were survivors of a wreck off the coast of New South Wales) and was very kind to the travel-worn refugees by 'filling their bellies and giving them many clothes'.

For many weeks they enjoyed the Governor's kind hospitality until the unfortunate appearance on September 17th. 1791, of Captain Edward Edwards — and then their secret was revealed because he knew the true story about their bold escape from Botany Bay. The nine escapees were now his prisoners to be returned to a British gaol.

He put them, shackled in irons, on board his ship 'Rembang' and they left Timor on October 6th. 1791, en route to Batavia. To be recaptured after all the hunger and suffering they had endured must have been painful.

En route to Batavia the 'Rembang' ran into a cyclone and its sails were torn to pieces by a terrifying storm which was accompanied by fierce thunder and lightning. By a miracle the ship was preserved from destruction and the Bryants, with their fellow prisoners, landed at Batavia under guard on November 7th. 1791.

They had to wait transportation to London via Capetown, but this naval port was regarded by seamen as a most unhealthy place and it was not long before seven of the ship's crew died. Tragically, Mary lost her little son, Emanuel, to the pestilence (dysentery or malaria) on December 1st. 1791, followed twenty-one days later by his father, William Bryant.

Sadly, on the way to Capetown, three more of the escaped convicts died — and when they arrived at the Cape in March, 1793, Mary, her surviving child, Charlotte, and the remaining four convicts were put on 'H.M.S. Gorgon' for their passage home to Britain.

On board the 'Gorgon' was a Marine Officer who had

travelled on the 'Charlotte' in 1787 and he at once recognized Mary and was familiar with her amazing escape. This Captain Trench later wrote: "I looked upon these people with pity and astonishment. To think they had failed in their heroic struggle for liberty, after having overcome every hardship and every difficulty."

Mary's cup of sorrow was not yet full, for on the way to England the 'Gorgon" encountered a period of hot weather and her little daughter, Charlotte, died.

The ship reached Portsmouth on June 18th. 1792, and that sorrowful mother with her four fellow-convicts was thrown into Newgate jail, in London — there to remain until the courts decided what punishment to give them.

The story of William and Mary Bryant excited the interest of London newspapers and their amazing adventure was printed under the title, "Wonderful Escape from Botany Bay". The article fully described their brave and desperate efforts to regain freedom by throwing themselves upon the mercy of the sea, rather than face the dread of starvation in a far-off land.

A certain barrister, James Boswell, was so impressed by the newspaper story that he felt Mary and her four companions should be granted a pardon — and so he offered to represent them in the Courts of Law without payment.

It was on May 2nd. 1793, that Mary Bryant (otherwise Broad) was granted a full pardon and set free to return to her own family in Fowey, Cornwall. That kind barrister not only provided for her return, but also sent more money to help her over the next few years. His sole condition was that "she behaved well". Did she? No one knows!

A hundred cashes with the cat-o'-nine tails

Natives hunting for their food

Mary Bryant

SHE WAS THE FIRST — AND THE LAST

Many Cornishmen and their families arrived here during the early 19th. Century to work in the copper mines of South Australia. In places such as Wallaroo, Kadina and Moonta the local cemeteries are full of Cornish folks who lived and toiled there many years ago.

Some eight thousand people have been buried in the Moonta cemetery — and there is a particularly morbid attraction here. Beside the large headstone of a miner, Thomas Woolcock who died aged 34 on September 4th. in 1873, visitors will see a small, unnamed grave which contains the body of his wife, Elizabeth Woolcock, the first and only woman to be hanged in South Australia.

Twenty-six-year-old Elizabeth stood trial for killing her husband by the administration of poison and was found guilty by a jury of twelve men who sentenced her to be hanged — but they added a recommendation for mercy because of her youth.

Over a period of weeks Elizabeth had administered doses of poison to her husband and had been unmoved by his suffering. Although three doctors had treated Thomas Woolcock while Elizabeth was feeding him poison, they had not diagnosed the cause of his illness — until there was a post-mortem.

Elizabeth's guilt was soon proved when police found she had purchased the poison from a chemist in Adelaide. However, Elizabeth confessed to the murder and in a written note published after she was hanged, tells a very sad story about her life.

She came to Burra Burra from Cornwall with her parents who then joined the gold rush to Victoria in 1851. When she was four years old her mother eloped with another man, deserting six young children. Her father died when she was nine and Elizabeth had to work as a kitchen maid — and while still a child she was raped by a Negro who was hanged for his crimes.

When she was eighteen she contacted her mother who invited Elizabeth to come and live with her and her second husband in Adelaide. Elizabeth was happy living with them and even became a Sunday school teacher in the local Wesleyan Church. Then she met Thomas Woolcock, a widower with two young boys, who offered to marry her so Elizabeth went to live with him in a miner's cottage near the North Yelta mine. But Thomas drank heavily, gave her very little money and beat her — and made her life so miserable that she tried to kill herself with poison. When that failed, she decided to get rid of the man who was ill-treating her. Can we really blame her?

Her stepfather advised strongly against it, but in a fit of obstinacy Elizabeth married the man, and went to live with him in a miner's cottage near the North Yelta mine, later known, with grim humour, as Poison Flat. She soon regretted her marriage; Thomas Woolcock drank heavily, expected her to keep house on half a crown a day, accused her of carrying on with a young man who boarded with them, and made her life so miserable that she tried to poison herself. When the attempt failed she decided to get rid of the man who was ill-treating her.

Although three doctors treated Thomas Woolcock in turn while Elizabeth was feeding him poison, they do not seem to have become suspicious until the post-mortem. Elizabeth's guilt was soon established through the purchase of the poison. She offered no defence worth mentioning, although a modern lawyer could have done a great deal for her by stressing how harshly life had dealt with her when she was young, her ignorance, and the misery of her married life.

Earliest picture of Moonta Mine–1862

The Cornish in South Australia

Burra, South Australia. Miners came to dig for copper.

SHE WAS THE FIRST — AND THE LAST

Thomas Pickett, a shepherd, discovered copper ore near the Burra creek in 1845 and soon the rush of miners from Cornwall began. By 1861 the Burra Burra mine employed 1,200 men. The old mine chimney in his photo shows 'Johnny Green', the miners' mascot, holding aloft his pick and gad.

A 'TITANIC" SURVIVOR DIES IN CORNWALL

Barbara Joyce Dainton became a well-known lady through no action of her own. In fact, she had no say ~ in the event that made her famous and has no recollection at all of the shocking affair as she was only ten months old at the time. Consequently, she always refused to talk about it because she felt that what happened was beyond her comprehension — and so it was.

Mrs. Dainton died in October, 2007, aged 96, in a Nursing Home in the town of Camborne, Cornwall. She was indeed widely-known as a survivor of R.M.S.'Titanic', yet she would never discuss the sea-tragedy that spawned at least two Hollywood films. She would say, *"I was only a babe in arms at the time, so I did not now what was happening around me on that fateful night Strangely, though, I've never liked ice in my drinks."*

The West family had boarded the "Titanic" at Southampton on Wednesday, 10th. April, 1912, to enjoy the liner's maiden voyage from England to America. It was the largest steamship afloat at that time and Mr. West had bought a family ticket for 27 pounds 15 shillings. The family's basic-type cabin was on C deck, amongst nearly 300 other second-class passengers.

However, after only four days at sea the "Titanic" struck an iceberg just before midnight on April 14th. 1912, and sank to the bottom of the North Atlantic Ocean. At first it was thought that little damage had been done to the great liner, but soon it was discovered the gigantic iceberg had ripped off great steel plates from the vessel's side so that she filled rapidly with water and went down in the middle of the night.

Barbara's father, 36 year-old Arthur West, drowned along with about 1520 other passengers and crew who were travelling on the "unsinkable" White Star liner — only 711 were saved.

In the arms of her pregnant mother (and accompanied by an older sister) Barbara was bundled into a lifeboat that was lowered into the sea in the darkness amidst great confusion and terror. There were not enough lifeboats for everyone so her father, like most of the men, went down with the ship.

"Women and children first" is the rule at sea when a ship is sinking and amongst the second-class passengers all twenty-four children were saved and more than half the women — but none of the men.

It was a bitterly-cold night and for several hours the survivors waited in their lifeboats until eventually they were picked up by the "Carpathia", a Cunard Liner. Those who

Barbara Dainton, at ten months old was one of the last remaining survivors on board the "Titanic", when she passed away, aged 96, in October 2007.

were swimming in the icy waters had little chance of surviving in such freezing conditions and by the time "Carpathia" arrived it was too late for the hundreds of floating, frozen corpses.

The surviving passengers were taken to New York and the West family returned to England on May 6th. About six months later, Mrs. West gave birth to a third daughter and both did surprisingly well considering the family's tragic loss of a husband and father.

Barbara was 41 when she married William Ernest Dainton. There were no children of the marriage and when her husband died Barbara retired to live in Truro, Cornwall. There she found satisfaction by working for several voluntary organisations — and she loved guiding visitors around the cathedral where she had donated a memorial tablet to her drowned father.

Truro Cathedral

R.M.S. Titanic,
In Memoriam, April 15, 1912.

She was not sunk *in* battle,
No tempest gave the shock,
She sprang no fatal leak,
She ran upon no rock.
'Titanic' was a wealthy ship
And thought to be unsinkable,
Until she hit an iceberg
And suffered the unthinkable.
God did not sink that liner;
'Twas just Man's carelessness
To let her steam at full speed
With such utter recklessness.
Across the icy waters

She sped without a care,
Yet each passenger on board
Would not be going anywhere.
Man's lack of due precaution
Meant she paid the highest price,
For she crashed into a mountain
That was made of solid ice.
With only sixteen lifeboats
It created quite a panic
As she sank beneath the waters
Of a freezing North Atlantic.
'Women and children, first!"
The life-boats soon were cast,
Yet fifteen hundred people drowned –
Though 'Carpathia' came fast.
And the ship's band calmly played,
"Nearer my God to Thee",
Until those brave musicians
Also sank beneath the sea.
Was Captain Smith responsible
For both his ship and crew?
They tell us that he shot himself,
Was that the proper thing to do?
— *Florence Breed.*

R.M.S. Titanic, In Memoriam, April 15, 1912.

A narrow street in St. Ives.

Ancient Milestone

Remnants of the tin-mining days.

Cornish Tales

St. Phillack Church

Stained glass window and high altar inside St. Gwinear Church.

A church sundial, Zennor.

R.M.S. Titanic, In Memoriam, April 15, 1912.

WHEELHOUSE

BOATS ON THE RIVER TAMAR

Cornish Tales

A Typical Cornish fishing village

R.M.S. Titanic, In Memoriam, April 15, 1912.

Morvah Church (Rebuit 1828)

Restormel Castle Ruins

Cornish Tales

Lands End

Newlyn

St. Sennara Church Zennor

R.M.S. Titanic, In Memoriam, April 15, 1912.

St Ives

Charlestown Harbour

A Cornish Cottage

Feock Creck

Bedruthan Steps, near Newquay

St. Michael's Mount (Marazion) near Penzance

R.M.S. Titanic, In Memoriam, April 15, 1912.

St. Agnes

Meragissey

Cotehele House

Polperro

Newlyn Harbour

Longships Lighthouse, Land's End

Love Quayside

R.M.S. Titanic, In Memoriam, April 15, 1912.

Mousehole Fishing Village

Tintagel Cove

St Ives

Village burned down by Spaniards.

Lanhydrock House

R.M.S. Titanic, In Memoriam, April 15, 1912.

St. Braddoc Church

Cornish Cross   St. Ives Church

Truro Cathedral
Roberts Memorial 1614

R.M.S. Titanic, In Memoriam, April 15, 1912.

Gwithian Church

Truro — Victoria Square

A 20TH. CENTURY CORNISH MISFIT ¿A SAD LETTER FROM A CORNISH MOTHER¿

I suppose I can't escape this letter to you, my dearest friend, without mention of our only son and heir. We are having dreadful problems with William. It's a long story, but in the end we decided we would have to part company, so we found a room for him in a boarding-house. We still love him, but we can't live with him. Of course, we are paying his rent, so I've had to take more hours at work to pay for it, though I'm pleased to say that at long last he has got another job.

Two months ago he had the sack from KFC. I just hope that now we are living apart we can build a better relationship together. I tried to phone him tonight, but he said he had a girlfriend there and did not want to have a conversation with me.

Hopefully he will contact us again. I hope and pray he will begin to "grow up". He was expelled from college and got into trouble with the police last month when he was brought home drunk in the middle of the night. He was getting into fights and was sacked from the DIY store where he worked.

He started to steal from us so often that I had to hide my money in a different place each day; and he was actively aggressive to both his sister and me whilst Tom was at work. He has run up a huge bill on our telephone and disabled the computer. Living with my son became absolute Hell — and his sister suffered a lot of bullying and aggression from him, too.

We took him to a therapist at thirty pounds an hour. It was a long journey to Truro from here, but William refused to co-operate with the specialist and in fact it made matters worse. He refused to take his medicine for his ADHD and became more disruptive and impulsive. So, at the moment we are paying hand over fist for a bit of peace in our home.

We both feel we have failed him as parents, but when I am away from him I realize that I had become frightened of his temper tantrums and angry outbursts. Now he has left home I do feel a lot calmer and happier.

There just seems to be no-one who can really help us and I could see that the specialist had no idea what to do with him. I had the impression that he blamed us for all that went wrong with our son.

I am even taking a job at a summer school at £25 a day, as a cleaner, but it definitely helps to pay some of William's: bills.

Actually he's not been, so bad lately, but we did have a 'phone call the other night. It was after midnight when we were all fast asleep in bed. William said he had been injured in a fight and would we come over immediately and drive him to the local hospital.

We were both very tired from decorating the kitchen and had ordered a take-away that evening, washed down with a bottle of red wine, so I told him I could not risk driving after drinking alcohol. He slammed the 'phone down in disgust which left us worrying where he was and what he was doing.

The phone rang again at 2-45 a.m. when he announced he was at the hospital (he'd called himself an ambulance) and even at the end of the phone we could hear him ranting and raving at the nurses. He was yelling at them and shouting that he'd been waiting for five hours and was bleeding to death.

I asked about his injuries and he said he'd got a nose bleed and a fat lip. Apparently, he had gone to the house of an ex-girlfriend and her father had hit him (which probably served him right). I can't help wondering if he had got the girl into trouble (you know what I mean) and that's why the father attacked him.

Well, then he slammed down the phone, but rang back again at 5-30 a.m. to say the hospital wouldn't treat him as it was only a small cut on the nose and a bruised lip. There was nothing the doctors could do, so the receptionist in the Casualty Department asked if we would go and pick him up. I imagine they were annoyed at all the commotion and fuss he was making. Tom went, bless him, and I think he gave William some 'strong words' on the way back.

William came here for dinner a couple of weeks ago which was difficult for me. I can't find it in my heart to truly forgive him for every bad thing he has done to us. I feel used and abused and I have told him that. Any length of time in his company is very hard for me. Until he apologises and talks about his problems we can't go forward together.

How can we forgive his aggressive attitude to us? To be honest, all the time he's not here everything is just fine and I feel as if a weight has been lifted off my shoulders.

Friends are so kind and sympathetic about our son. It's hard — oh, so hard. My heart is breaking. He came again today to pick up some of his gear, but that kid is so arrogant and mixed-up.

Tom is very kind and patient. He tries to talk to him, but William will not listen. He has only worked for five days in five weeks, so we had to pay his rent again for another two weeks (£110) We are very much in debt now because of it all, yet I suppose it soothes our consciences to help him in this way. I hate to say it, but it's so peaceful when he's not here that we would willingly pay his rent to keep him away permanently.

He has enough food now for a few weeks which I bought and took around to him. I tried to get some help from Social Services, the Job Centre and Housing Commission, but none of them wanted to know about him. It seems as long as we can afford to pay everything for him they don't want to know about our troubles.

Last month he had a job in a cafe, but it only lasted one day because he took the rest of the week off and, naturally, the owner sacked him. Now he starts another job next Monday at a Nursing Home, but I don't think he'll last the pace there. I sent him a Good Luck card tonight telling him we love him. Perhaps it was the wrong thing to do as he'll probably just laugh at my foolish sentimentality.

Where did we go wrong with William!? His sister has never been any trouble — a perfect student at school and keen on golf and tennis so we have always encouraged her sporting hobbies. But William was never interested in sport, or anything else we suggested he might like to do.

Did I tell you that William actually pulled a knife on me once in the kitchen, but fortunately at that very moment Tom's uncle telephoned and somehow I kept calm enough to persuade William to talk to Tom's uncle. That wonderfully-understanding man calmed him down over the phone. It gave me enough time to escape from the house and I was so frightened that I locked myself in the garden shed until Tom came home.

It is really difficult for me when we visit Tom's relatives and I don't actually enjoy those days very much as I feel so sensitive about William They keep saying they have had the same problems themselves with their children, but always managed to deal with them successfully.

They don't really know anything of what went on between us and William and to talk about it makes me feel extremely upset and weepy so I can never tell them the whole sequence of terrible events. But it is very galling when they flippantly tell me that all teenagers can be difficult with their own problems; and that William is really no different from any other modern child.

They will never know what traumas we have been through — and I don't particularly want to tell them, either. The moment that you start to talk about our problem to the family they just wave their hands in the air and turn it around by saying that we just don't know how to cope with him and don't understand him. They remark that Nature is trying to tell people something when they can't have children of their own; therefore, such people are foolish to adopt. Now, I find that comment is very cruel, as all we ever really tried to do was to give him a loving home.

Now, whenever they ask about William I just grit my teeth, smile graciously, and say he's doing quite well. To which they reply, "Surely things were never as bad as you said, were they? It's just because you did not know how to handle him; and now that he's away from you, he's fine." They make irritating comments to Tom like, "Lin always seems so tense! She should not be so highly-strung!"

Did I mention that Rosemary (the woman who was living with William and is much older than he) has left him and moved into a new flat on her own. We have spoken to her and she seems very happy, although she won't tell us why she left William. I guess we have our own suspicions about that.

He has just lost another job and says he's been busy having

interviews, but cannot get any job; so we've sent him money as he yelled he can't manage to live on £150 a week with all his bills.

I'm afraid I rather lost my temper with him when he asked for more money and I explained to him that his dad didn't bring home an awful lot more than that and we managed on it quite well — running a house and two cars and feeding three people. But then again we don't drink, or smoke, or go out anywhere.

I often wonder if it is because Tom is a policeman (a sergeant) that William feels he can get into trouble with the Law and somehow get away with it? Is it because his father is always there at the local Police Station to bail him out? I wish I knew the answer to William's aggressive attitude. Is it something we failed to do for him in the past?"

My poor friend and her husband were unable to have children of their own so adopted a boy and a girl from Dr. Barnardo's Orphanage. They never told the children and thought their secret would remain hidden for ever. Unfortunately, when he was twelve years old, William found out that he had been adopted — and ever since has been nothing but trouble. Perhaps this sad situation proves that children should be told the truth about their real parentage at a very early age — before they hear it accidentally from other people.

This selfish young man appears to be a sad product of our modern times as he is involved heavily in drugs and alcohol abuse. Should we blame television, computers and the materialistic age in which we live? And who can find a cure for this young man's aggressive, anti-social and ungrateful behaviour?

CORNISH MEMORIES OF AN EVACUEE

It was after the German attack on Poland that France and Great Britain declared war (3rd. September, 1939). At first it was a "phoney war" for us as nothing much happened until the Spring of 1940 when my home in Plymouth came under attack from the Luftwaffe.

We survived many of the Air-Raids, huddling each night inside our little Anderson shelter in the back garden. But near the end of 1943 an unexploded landmine fell into the neighbour's garden and we had to leave our house. My brother and I caught a train to West Cornwall to stay with my father's elderly cousins in the parish where my parents (and generations of ancestors) had once lived.

It was taken for granted that two town kids would soon fit into the age-old routine of Cornish rural life. Unfortunately, the village children regarded evacuees as "furriners" and my parents had always protected me from children who were rough. But I was on my own now.

These rough children threw words like stones and wore torn clothes revealing bare thighs They ran about the street all day and climbed garden walls and washed at the village-well. They sprang out from behind hedges, barking like mad dogs — and they threw mud.

As town-evacuees we found ourselves transported from civilization into a past era of dim candles, gloomy oil lamps and water in buckets. The toilet was an earth-closet at the end of a long garden where fowls scratched amongst the blackcurrant bushes and potato plants. The cottage where we lived with cousin Maud and her husband was once the home of my great-grandfather Henry Skewes. He was promoted to Mine Manager in 1852 and the villagers called him "Cap'en Skewes".

In those days, copper and tin miners slaved in subterranean tunnels.

A typical Cornish "privy" looked like a long wooden box with a hole cut out of the top over which one was expected to sit without falling through into the deep cess-pit beneath. Torn squares of newspaper beside one's right hand completed the necessary, hygienic requirements.

To a city child who was only used to buildings and streets,

those tall hedgerows were fascinating, especially where the tiny red robins built their nests amongst the thickest brambles beyond the reach of egg-stealing boys. There were the sweet-smelling, pink flowers of the hawthorn bush and the shining-black berries of the elder tree, but my favourite was "Old Man's Beard" whose fluffy, white festoons adorned the hedge-tops on frosty Autumn mornings.

At the northern end of Reawla I had to pass several houses inhabited by the roughest boys I had ever seen and it was a most frightening experience to run their gauntlet of stones. These boys possessed an uncanny sixth sense, for as soon as an outsider like myself came within shouting distance they would emerge, uttering war cries that terrified me and lent wings to my feet.

This same gang of thugs would often hide amongst the disused mine shafts of Relistian, ready to jump out and pelt me with turfs as I passed on my way to school. I often had to run the gauntlet of their hate, but somehow I managed to run faster than they could with their big, clumsy boots and ill-fitting trousers.

I believe, in times gone by, it was a Cornish custom for people to throw stones at strangers. It was said that as late as 1850 a miner in Breage and Sithney could hardly pass from his own parish to another without danger of being assaulted and maltreated. Even a funeral procession moving from one parish to another was assailed with showers of stones. Consequently, as Sunday was held to be a day of truce it became the custom to hold funerals on a Sunday.

I never objected to being sent to bed for I always took a book with me to read by candle-light under the blankets and it was a miracle I never set fire to the bed.

Cousin Dennis was a fine-looking man, an agricultural

labourer, lean and strong. He could devour in one sitting a pasty as long and round as the largest dinner plate.

He had been to the war, driving horses that pulled heavy ammunition waggons through the Somme mud and bullets and at the end of that terrible conflict he returned home as deaf as a post though still a young man in years.

Dennis was very kind. On winter nights as we sat around the coal fire he would tell me about his boyhood and the tricks he used to play to frighten other folks in the village, [It always seemed to me that they made up their own fun in order to get the better of someone else.]

In Gwinear-village the little terraced-houses had their front doors close together, so Dennis and his friends would creep along the street tying door-handles together; then they would knock on the doors before hiding to watch the fun.

As villagers tried to open their doors they found them immovable and the more they tugged from inside the funnier it must have seemed to the watchers outside.

One time, Dennis put a sheet around himself and rode through the village on a "borrowed" donkey. It was a dark, stormy night and old women peeping from their windows were frightened out of their wits. [The Cornish were very prone to seeing ghosts and really took them seriously.]

Another trick was to hide behind tombstones in the chuchyard and jump out to frighten some passer-by.

Cousin Dennis would also sing songs from the First World War, tear-drops shining at the corner of each eye as his voice trembled with emotion. His favourites were "Mademoiselle from Armentieres, parlez vous?" and "Pack up your troubles in your old kit bag".

When he recalled jokes he played on people in his youth, he would laugh till the tears ran down his face. Sometimes he would pretend to read my name out of his newspaper, (Perhaps his was the last generation to maintain old Cornish customs)

In today's sophisticated world such simple jokes and pastimes would appear elementary and foolish, but it was a Cornish tradition to make fun by creating one's own amusements and it certainly showed admirable inventiveness on their part.

This was the old way of life in Cornish villages, an attitude that still existed when I was living there. Perhaps neighbours were jealous of each other, constantly watching each other and wanting to take each other down a peg or two.

I soon realised that local gossip was the very life-blood of this Cornish village and there was always plenty of it because everybody knew everybody else's business. Cousin Maud warned me to keep away from those village women who stood at their gates all day long to observe everybody's movements. But this inquisitive way of life was the same for my parents, and their parents before them.

Mother told me how they had to provide their own entertainment in the days when there were no cinemas, no radio, no television, no telephones and no gadding about in buses and cars. With musical concerts, dressing-up and the playing of practical jokes, young men and women made their own fun.

   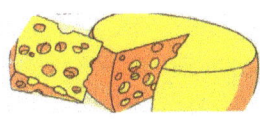   

Crocus (saffron)   *Cheese (and bread for supper)*   *goose*

The road into the village and town was no more than six feet wide and on each side "hedges" formed a protective barrier from the wind and rain. A Cornish hedge is like a wall, made from half-stone and half-earth, varying from six to ten feet high and about two feet broad; and long before the invention of macadam roads Cornish folks were obliged to walk along the top of the hedges making a narrow path there, because often there was no other road and thus they avoided a muddy walk across ploughed fields.

Cornwall was once known as "The Land of Giants" and, perhaps that myth arose when visitors to this treeless county could see in the misty-light people as tall as trees ~ and did not realise they were looking at ordinary folks who were walking on tops of hedges in order to keep out of the oozing, thick mud that covered walking-tracks and lanes. Obviously, the tops of hedges made dry, alternative, walking-routes.

As soon as these stone — hedges were made it did not take long before Cornwall's wet, temperate climate encouraged a luxurious plant growth that bound loose stones and earth together, creating a green oasis in which birds, plants and small animals might thrive unmolested.

At "Henver Farm" each day the morning break for the workers consisted of broth served in huge bowls at the long kitchen table. Lilian Harvey, the farmer's sister, would make a thin broth from vegetables, mainly leeks, and this dish of good broth was looked upon as an excellent source of nourishment, very satisfying for hungry farm labourers when served with freshly-baked bread.

During my stay I noticed that those inclined towards godliness would wash in a large tin-bath, but most Cornish folks considered that washing "bits" of the body was quite sufficient and for that purpose I had a large china bowl with matching jug on a marble stand in my bedroom.

Such traditional country habits did not change until the end of the Second World War when working-class people were better-off.

After an invigorating walk home from the village school in the face of a Nor'wester blowing in from the Atlantic Ocean, there is no more delicious aroma than that of freshly-baked potato scones and heavy cake. In those days the women stayed at home, cleaning, washing and baking for their large families. There were no shops nearby and the big stores in Camborne Town were not easily accessible to villagers until the early 1940's when buses began to appear in these outlying areas.

It was not until the advent of easy transport that the more intrepid villagers ventured further afield to do their shopping, which meant the death of each village-shop and gradually everyone began to experience the replacement of traditional, home-baked recipes with "boughten" foods from the many fascinating stores in town.

A loaf of fresh bread, home-baked, thickly-sliced and spread with home-made blackberry jam is an unforgettable experience; and until recent years the genuine Cornish housewife could make bread and yeast buns with an ease inherited from generations of experience.

A cold walk home from school always produced a healthy appetite and, though it may seem humble fare to more sophisticated palates, there is nothing more delicious and satisfying than bread baked in a Cornish oven and eaten in the warmth of a small kitchen whilst the rain beats down upon the slate roof and trickles across the tiny window-panes. In Cornwall it rains pretty well all winter, with very little frost or snow, but there is rain and storms aplenty.

One traditional cake that our domestic servant, Mary Jane, could bake better than anyone else was "Heavy cake" and I would look forward to her "cooking days" just to get a piece of this much-desired food.

"Heavy cake" when made up lightly by a good cook such as Mary Jane, is by no means as indigestible as its name sounds and was always my favourite food at tea-time.

It is composed of flour mixed with butter and sour cream, with a handful of currants and a pinch of salt. The butter is rubbed into the flour and then made into a dough by adding sour cream. The dough is rolled out flat to a thickness of about one inch and then lightly scored with a knife into diamond shapes before being baked in a hot oven.

I was soon introduced to marinated pilchards with bread and butter and strong, brewed tea. This was very much enjoyed as a savoury meal by my Cornish cousins who would often have a dish of pilchards, chopped up with raw onions and salt.

The first time I tasted marinated pilchards I choked on their fine, sharp bones and vowed never to touch them again, but Cousin Maud and her husband had been reared on pilchards and ate them with their fingers in true Cornish fashion.

For centuries the humble pilchard has been the chief support of ordinary folks who considered it their greatest delicacy. Each fishing season, a hawker from the little fishing port of Porthleven would arrive.

[Amazing to think that during the 1800's Cornish folks could buy as many as a hundred pilchards just for sixpence.]

The fish were laid with plenty of salt inside a large earthenware pot known as a "bussa" and in this they could be safely stored for months. The "bussa" stood behind the jammed and never-used front door. When required for tea, the pilchards were washed and placed in a baking dish with vinegar, spices and bay leaves, and then left to cook slowly in the Cornish oven.

Each morning before walking to school, I had to fetch a can of milk from the neighbouring farm and I dreaded having to pass a ferocious gaggle of geese whose hissing leader obviously disliked me.

If the old gander was busy feeding I could pass unnoticed, but usually he was waiting behind the gate with outstretched neck and wings and open beak ready to strike. Running to escape his vicious attacks I would spill some of the milk and then I had to face a stern reprimand from cousin Maud.

At Christmas-time I was quite happy to see the farmer plucking his hissing devils to sell for the villagers' Christmas dinners as country folks love nothing better than the taste of roast goose on special occasions.

The farmer's sister was not too fussy about her personal habits and it sometimes worried me to see her using her hands to churn the butter or to skim the rich crust of cream from the top of the huge pans of milk, yet we never had any symptoms of food poisoning.

I soon became addicted to that traditional Cornish food known as "saffron cake" — there is nothing to compare with it. Mother used to speaks fondly about Sunday School Picnics in her youth when each child received a big saffron bun as part of the treat.

They say that ancient Phoenicians brought saffron powder to Cornwall and ever since the Cornish have clung to it and carried it to every corner of the globe with them.

Saffron originally came from a real plant. It is the deliciously-scented extract of the crocus flower.

Cousin Maud had a great liking for "seedy buns" which are yeast buns flavoured with caraway seeds and much appreciated in Cornwall, though not by me. It is the only Cornish food I truly dislike.

It was not necessary for a Cornish woman to read a recipe because her baking skills were purely practical ones that had been handed down, unchanged and unchangeable, from generation to generation.

"Cornish stew" was always my favourite meal. It was made with huge amounts of potatoes, turnips and onions, to which a small amount of beef was added if the war-rations permitted it, but the best part of "Cornish stew" was the mouth-watering dumplings made from flour and suet.

Stew must be cooked slowly in an iron pot over the fire for this makes the stew thick and tasty. Often rabbits were put in the stew. Known as "the poor man's chicken" this poor, maligned creature has freely provided the only source of meat for generations of Cornish people. Rabbits are caught with traps set around the fields at the bottom of the hedges. These "Gins" had steel jaws that closed with a vicious snap, breaking the leg of the rabbit ~ and sometimes I could hear from my bedroom the squeals of agony made by a rabbit caught in a gin.

Mother told me they lived on rabbits when she was a child in Cornwall and I often saw father eating the cooked white brains and tiny tongue which he regarded as great delicacies.

Sometimes a special treat for supper was a big saffron bun (baked by the village woman who came to do housework for cousin Maud) with a cup of cocoa each — a rare treat indeed considering ingredients such as flour, butter and sugar were severely rationed during the war.

Customs and routine changed quickly with the arrival

CORNISH MEMORIES OF AN EVACUEE

St. Gwinear, 1901. My father (aged 11) helps his blind uncle to deliver sacks of coal to the villagers.

THE SHOP HAS GONE BECAUSE NOW PEOPLE HAVE CARS TO CARRY THEM EVERYWHERE. THEY NO LONGER HAVE TO STAY IN THE VILLAGE, BUT CAN GO ANYWHERE THEY PLEASE.

of public buses and villagers could now visit Camborne's skating-rink, hotels, pubs, cafes, restaurant, dance-hall and cinema. Lively Hollywood movies provided a new kind of entertainment that attracted many people into the nearby town where they would gaze hypnotically at handsome Hollywood actors and actresses on the silver screen.

333

The rural scene changed dramatically as soon as villagers spent their spare time and entertainment further afield. The old days were disappearing fast; yet let us not forget that mining, fishing and farming were once the only three industries that kept Cornwall alive, so here is an old Cornish song that sums up those three occupations: -

Farmers with their breeches on
Their boots filled up with straw.
Miners with their pick and gad
And powder for to blow.
The more the miners sing
The more farmers fill their quarts.
The more the sailors sink
The more the aching hearts.

St. Gwinear mining village ~ today

"Come-to-Good" is the place of the first Quaker Meeting-House in Cornwall (built in 1710)

GEORGE FOX (1624-91) was the founder of the "Society of Friends" and as a youth he spent much time in reading the Bible. Then in 1647 he heard a voice which said, "There is one, even Christ Jesus, that can speak to thy condition," and these words gave him the message which he proclaimed throughout his life. His travels took him all over Britain and twice to Europe and America. Fox was big and strong in appearance, with piercing eyes and long hair. He spoke against the priests who were paid to preach and who lacked divine learning and proclaimed that the church is the body of Christians and not the building in which they worship, which he called a 'steeple-house'. He used the plain 'thee and thou' to all men whatever their class in society. In 1652 the large groups of his followers in Swarthmore, Westmoreland, used the home of the Judge Fell family and it became the centre of Fox's great missionary movement. Fox preached that Christ has conquered sin and that man need only to turn to Him and be obedient to His voice and He will give him victory over sin. Fox paved the way for John Wesley's message in the next century. (The Friends' Meeting-House in Plymouth is called, 'Swarthmore Hall'.)

NEWS FROM CORNWALL

In these unhappy times with the world so much changed after the terrorist attacks of 11th. September, it can be a pleasant distraction to hear newsworthy stories from my home county.

Only last month, in a little Cornish village called Bere Ferrers, a special remembrance service was held to honour a group of Anzacs who died there during World War 1. I know this place because it is only seven miles from Plymouth and Mother used to take us there for picnics when we were children.

Of course, one wonders why a group of Anzacs went to that obscure village in the first place and what happened to them there.

Well, it seems that on the 24th. September, 1917, a big contingent of Australians and New Zealanders disembarked at Devonport Docks, near Plymouth. The soldiers then boarded a special troop-train to carry them northwards to camps on Salisbury Plain where they would receive a course of preliminary training in preparation for the battlefields of France.

Before their train left Plymouth, a group of soldiers was detailed by an officer to pick up food supplies waiting for them on the platform at Exeter Railway Station. However, the rocking sensation of the moving train sent these exhausted soldiers to sleep until they were rudely awakened when the train shuddered to a grinding halt just outside Bere Ferrers village.

The ten soldiers who had been ordered to collect the food

parcels, not knowing the area, thought they had arrived in Exeter so immediately jumped off the train.

It was a moonless night and while the sleepy soldiers were still standing on the railway lines another train making its way from Waterloo to Plymouth came into Bere Ferrers station. The London engine-driver did not see the soldiers slowly moving along the tracks until the very last moment — and was unable to stop in time.

It was an horrific and tragic accident, but the troop-train had to continue on its way without delay for there was a war on. The kindly villagers of Bere Ferrers took care of those poor, mangled bodies and buried them with due respect in the local churchyard. Ever since that day, eighty-four years ago, local people have been carefully tending the soldiers' graves.

The dead Australians and New Zealanders were only young men in their early 20's. They lie far away from home and loved ones; therefore, it is good to know that a permanent memorial now stands in this little village to honour them and also to let future generations know about their sacrifice.

I wonder if 12,000 miles away on this side of the world anyone thinks of them? At least, it is comforting to know that the people of Bere Ferrers do.

Memorial for Anzacs in Bere Ferrers village, Cornwall. Soldier Heroes of the First Wold War

HEROISM IN NEW YORK – 2001

What a refreshing change to hear about decent people instead of terrorists and their deeds of evil! Stories are now emerging about countless acts of heroism committed inside the burning, collapsing, twin towers of New York's World Trade Centre on September 11th.

We hear how during that terrible day many wonderful people were prepared to lay down their lives to save others, so let us forget the murderers, morons and maniacs for a moment and think about the selfless, generous members of our human race.

One such person was a Cornishman, Rick Rescorla, who worked in the World Trade Centre as head of a security firm. His offices were on the 42nd. floor of the vast building.

Many survivors from the horror of that terrorist onslaught bear witness to the actions of Rick Rescorla; and there is no doubt that while we were watching the horrifying consequences of that mad attack on our television screens, Cornishman Rick Rescorla was giving his own life to save thousands of others.

The last photograph taken of Rick Rescorla by a passing workmate shows him speaking through a megaphone as he guides people to safety. He could easily have saved himself, but instead he stayed behind to ensure that the workers in his department would escape the blazing inferno. As a result of his courage and unflappability he saved hundreds of lives. Eyewitnesses tell the story of how he guided them down the stairs and calmed everyone with music, for he was a good singer, and he sang to them the traditional Cornish songs of his childhood.

There was the "Helston Floral Dance" song with a foot-tapping, rollicking rhythm; Cornwall's rousing national anthem, "Trelawney"; the cheerful "Obby Oss" song from Padstow; and "Up Camborne Hill, Coming Down". The last-named song proves to me he came from my part of West Cornwall because only the locals really know that one!

At the final count, about six colleagues in his security firm and himself failed to make it out of the wreckage. We know this son of Cornwall was a hero because of the unique and unusual circumstances surrounding his death, but as we think of his last brave actions during that terrible atrocity we might also remember the 4,000 or more other victims that died there, too.

Cyril Richard Rescorla was born in Hayle, Cornwall, in 1939 and as a young lad in 1943 he watched U.S. soldiers of the 29th. Infantry Division use this seaside town for their army practice and temporary home. Young Rescorla admired the Yanks and wanted to become a soldier just like them.

RICK RESCORLA — moments before he died. (Photo: 'Cornish Western Morning News')
A Cornish Hero of the Twenty-first century

OLD CORNWALL AND ITS MINERS

"Wherever there's a hole in the ground," runs an old saying, "you'll find a Cousin Jack at the bottom of it, searching for metal."

It was the work of all Cornishmen, across many centuries, to dig for metal in the land of their birth. The tin deposits of that little English county were first worked four thousand years ago — and in the Middle Ages Cornwall became very important as the main source of tin throughout the Ancient World. By 1450 B.C. Cornish tin was sold as far away as the Aegean Sea — and the great seafarers of that day, such as the Phoenicians and the Romans, came to Cornwall to buy tin direct.

Down through the ages, tin mining was an important industry of Cornwall, until the discovery of copper in Cornwall in 1703. Finding copper deposits involved digging deep shafts and tunnels and this gave miners even more opportunities for work It is not surprising then that when the mines of Cornwall closed down in the late 1800's because of overseas competition — it was a case of "Emigrate, or stay and starve!"

Cornish miners (many amongst my own family ancestors) decided to emigrate to other countries which required their expert mining skills — places such as the U.S.A., Mexico, South Africa, South America, Canada, New Zealand and Australia.

These miners and their families took with them to their new country all their old manners and customs, especially their traditional sports and pastimes. The women continued to bake their Cornish pasties, saffron buns and sesame cakes and cockfighting continued as it had done in Cornwall for centuries.

In South Australia, cockfighting did not last long after the coming of the Salvation Army's religious revival. It was a cruel sport and eventually was banned in all countries. However, the Cornish took their ancient sport of wrestling everywhere and games were contested by some of the best wrestlers out of Cornwall.

However, nothing ever stays the same and eventually wrestling was replaced by foot-racing which attracted big crowds everywhere it occurred. Later, horse-racing became popular — and then by the 1870's cricket matches became the favourite sport.

Sweat and tears: a South Crofty miner
Cornish tin-mining ends

('The Western Morning News, August, 1997.)

THE LAST working tin mine in Cornwall is to close, ending an industry that dates back many centuries.

South Crofty, near Camborne, the only commercial tin mine in Europe, has become a victim of falling tin prices and the strong pound.

The Crew Group, its Canadian owner, said operations would cease gradually over the next six months after which the miles of tunnels would be allowed to flood.

The closure will make 275 people redundant and have a knock-on effect on the Cornish economy.

"I realise the history of tin-mining in Cornwall and this is a dreadful day," said David Giddings, the mine's managing director. "It was a depressing decision to have to make but it was the only option. The mine does not have a commercial future.

"We need to close it now. Another month's losses would mean we would not have enough money to pay the wages and redundancy payments."

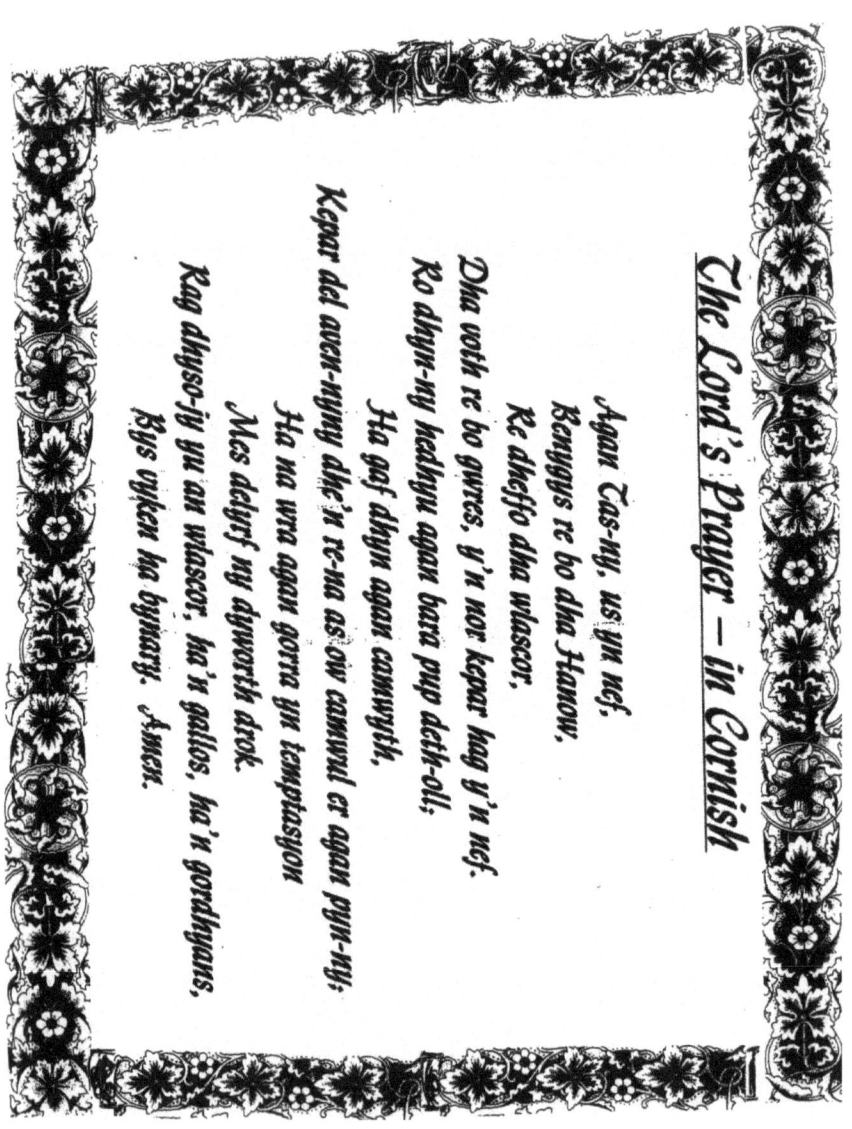

The Lord's Prayer – in Cornish

Agan Tas-ny, usi yn nef,
Benygys re bo dha Hanow,
Re dheffo dha wlascor,
Dha voth re bo gwres, y'n nor kepar hag y'n nef.
Ro dhyn-ny hedhyu agan bara pup dedh-oll;
Ha gaf dhyn agan camwyth,
Kepar del aven-nyny dhe'n re-na as ow camwul er agan pyn-ny;
Ha na wra agan gorra yn temptasyon
Mes delyrf ny dyworth drok.
Rag dhyso-jy an wlascor, ha'n gallos, ha'n gordhyans,
Bys vyken ha bynary. Amen.

A CORNISH POET: Charles Causley

Born in 1917, in Launceston, Cornwall, Charles Causley attended the village school and then studied to become a teacher. He lived with his widowed mother while teaching at the local village school. He began writing poetry and was well-known later as a "children's poet". His first
poems were published in 1951 and he was often invited to speak at various English teachers' conferences. He never married and when he died in 2003 at the age of 86 he was buried beside his mother in Launceston Churchyard.

Launceston Village School

Timothy Winters

Timothy Winters comes to school
With eyes as wide as a football-pool,
Ears like bombs and teeth like splinters :
A blitz of a boy is Timothy Winters.
His belly is white, his neck is dark,
And his hair is an exclamation-mark.
His clothes are enough to scare a crow
And through his britches the blue winds blow.
When teacher talks he won't hear a word
And he shoots down dead the arithmetic-bird,
He licks the patterns off his plate
And he's not even heard of the Welfare State.
Timothy Winters has bloody feet
And he lives in a house on Suez Street,
He sleeps in a sack on the kitchen floor
And they say there aren't boys like him any more.
Old Man Winters likes his beer
And his missus ran off with a bombardier,
Grandma sits in the grate with a gin
And Timothy's dosed with an aspirin.

—Charles Causley

Sir John Betjeman

Born 28 August, 1906
Died 19 May, 1984
(aged 77)
Buried
St. Enadoc Church.
Cornwall
(*from 'the Western Morning News'*)

John Betjeman's grave

POET LAUREATE

Seaside Golf
How straight it flew, how long it flew,
It clear'd the rutty track
And soaring, disappeared from view
Beyond the bunker's back –
A glorious, sailing, bounding drive
That made me glad I was alive.

And down the fairway, far along
It glowed a lonely white;
I played an iron sure and strong
And clipp'd it out of sight,
And spite of grassy banks between
I knew I'd find it on the green.

And so I did. It lay content
Two paces from the pin;
A steady putt and then it went
Oh, most securely in.
The very turf rejoiced to see
That quite unprecedented three.

Celebrating Cornwall's Mining History

In July 2006, Cornwall and West Devon's rich mining heritage was recognised when the region was designated a UNESCO World Heritage Site, placing the county's ruined engine houses on an equal footing with The Pyramids and the Taj Mahal. To celebrate the 10th anniversary of this recognition, a series of events took place during July and August 2016 featuring the largest mechanical puppet ever built — the "Man Engine".

This mechanical monster made his way across the mining heritage sites — starting at Tavistock and finishing a week later amid the iconic ruined mine chimneys which dot the landscape in the area around Geevor Tin Mine on the far west coast of Cornwall.

The Man Engine is a giant mechanical representation of a tin miner, animated by a crew of puppeteers dressed as miners and "bal-maidens", women who worked above ground sorting the ore. It is the creation of puppet master Hal Sylvester, along with Will Coleman, who narrates the show. During the hour-long ceremony, the Man Engine was raised up to a height of almost 40 feet, amid a whirring of wheels and spouting steam. Throughout the show, local musicians perform specially written songs reflecting Cornish mining culture.

The term "Man Engine" originally referred to the steam-powered winding mechanism used to lower and raise the miners in their journey to and from the tunnels deep underground. At Wheal Owles mine near Levant in 1919, a tragedy

Celebrating Cornwall's Mining History

The Man Engine makes his way through Lostwithiel, Cornwall.

occurred when a failure of the mechanism led to the death of 31 miners who were just approaching the surface.

At last we have an impressive way to remember all those miners who were killed while digging for tin and copper in Cornwall. Many of these miners died young from "miner's lung" as it was called, so Cornwall was known as the "Land of Widows" and there were no pensions or recompense for their families from the rich mine owners.

This is the largest mechanical puppet ever built and known as the "Cornish Man Mining Engine". It stands over 30 feet tall and is manipulated by operators pulling ropes. The puppet's rocking neck resembles a giant beam engine and the hands are like modern excavators. It will travel through Cornwall for all to see, but a bit late for my ancestors.

The puppet, topped with a safety helmet, is a tribute to the miners of Cornwall

THE MIGHTY MINER

HUMPHREY DAVY — born Penzance 1778.
One of the greatest of British chemists. In 1815 he invented the miner's safety lamp. He died in 1829 in Geneva.

RICHARD TREVITHICK — born Camborne 1771.
A great inventor and engineer in the mining industry. He applied high-pressure steam to winding and pumping engines and invented the world's first railway locomotive which ran in South Wales in 1804. He died in 1833 while working in Dartford, Kent, and was buried at his workmates' expense.

A CHILD OF THE BLITZ

It was 1943 and Germany was definitely winning the war, so Christmas at the end of that year was not a good time for celebration. Cornwall was lucky to escape Hitler's bombs, but just across the River Tamar, during those early years of 1940 and 1941, the city of Plymouth had the distinction of being the most bombed city outside London.

Canterbury, Liverpool, Coventry, Portsmouth, Bristol, Southampton Exeter and Swansea suffered intense bombing raids, but the Luftwaffe destroyed most of my city until little remained of it as it was in the days of Sir Francis Drake, its most famous son.

"Have you ever been to Plymouth? It was a lovely seaside place before the war started, But now you would be brokenhearted if you saw the mess German planes made. Night after night they flew overhead making me jump from my warm, cozy bed And run to the Anderson shelter in haste, while houses collapsed and streets laid waste. Buildings just crumbled everywhere — it was cruel, yet people showed no fear."

I wrote these lines a long time ago to remind myself what life was like after the upheaval of the Blitz in 1940 and '41. The reason Hitler unleashed the full fury of his Luftwaffe upon cities was to weaken people's resistance — thus he hoped to enter London in triumph before another year could pass. By 1942 the enemy was on England's doorstep because Germany had already overrun six countries — Poland, Denmark, Norway, Holland, Belgium and France. However, to achieve an invasion of Britain, Hitler had to rely upon his bombers to prepare the way — but his airmen would soon learn that the ability of our British fighter pilots was greater than theirs and that our 'Spitfires' and 'Hurricanes' were more than a match for Germany's 'Messerschmitts' and 'Heinkels'.

Shop windows were empty at Christmas, except for cardboard imitation chocolates and jars of realistic-looking paper sweets. My brother and I were not evacuated until later in the war because Mum said, "If we are going to die, we will all die together." Altogether Plymouth had 59 bombing raids with a cost of nearly 2,000 civilians killed and almost 4,000 injured.

In Christmas 1942 we had little reason to celebrate the Festive Season because Hitler was definitely winning the war. It certainly wasn't fun having bombs dropped on us and having all our windows blown out and the roof-tiles smashed. On Christmas Day the churches were packed as people knelt to pray for Peace and an end to their suffering. (Does it really take a war to persuade folks to attend church?)

My father was in charge of naval security so we had no choice but to live close to the Devonport Dockyard. During the following weeks of that sunny September in 1939, I watched Dad and his naval pal, digging a great hole in our back garden in which to put the Anderson Air-Raid shelter. They dug a pit deep enough to stand up in and long enough for people to lie down in — and wide enough for a couple of camp beds. Their hardest part was lifting the heavy, curved, steel sheets into the big hole. Then they covered the shelter with about 15 inches of earth, so it was well-camouflaged from the air and would just look like a big brown igloo.

I remember that Dad offered to return the favour and help his naval pal put a shelter in his garden, but he refused, saying he would rather stay in bed, during an Air-Raid because if he was going to be blown up he might as well die in comfort.

A CHILD OF THE BLITZ

American soldiers flooded Cornwall to practise for the D-Day landings – 1944

Man of a thousand quips – world-famous American comedian Bob Hope rallies American troops at Bodmin, summer, 1943

The scene of devastation at the City Hospital. Fourteen babies and three nurses died

Top: American soldiers flooded Cornwall to practise for the D-Day landings — 1944
Middle: The scene of devastation at the City Hospital. Fourteen babies and three nurses died
Left: The ruins of a main street in Plymouth's city centre

A gang of rescue workers pauses for a group photograph amidst the ruins of what was once Cornwall Street in the city centre

At first Dad planted flowers on top, but later he decided it would be a good growing space for carrots, lettuces and radishes. Posters everywhere told people to "Dig for Victory", but the inventor of those garden shelters, Sir John Anderson, was not amused, saying he had not intended his steel shelters to be used in such a way.

By the time Christmas arrived we were quite accustomed to shouts of, *"Put that Light Out!"* echoing along the street after dusk. Mother had sewn yards of thick, black material to cover all our windows and doors. Then she carefully stuck diagonal strips of wide tape across every glass pane to prevent flying splinters caused by bomb-blast. These precautions had been recommended by the government and were enforced once the war actually started with hefty fines for anyone found guilty of disobeying them.

The Government gave us a free Anderson shelter because we lived in a certified danger zone as our house was very close to Devonport Dockyard where destroyers and cruisers were being built, or refitted for the war. For the protection of people who had no private shelters, there were scores of public ones built in various streets. However, even these were no guarantee against a direct hit and one of the biggest losses occurred when a bomb landed on a large shelter in the city centre killing at least 72 people. No bodies were ever recovered as they were all blown to pieces.

I remember the bright searchlights that raked the skies each night — and those huge, gas-filled, barrage balloons that floated above us as a protection from enemy planes. Whenever a damaged balloon fell to the ground, women would scramble to pick up the pieces and make them into garments. My mother made a blouse for me from a piece of that silver material.

In school we used to practise putting on our gas masks — but wearing those rubber-masks made us look like little black pigs. They were very tight and suffocating because they completely covered the face. We also practised marching in orderly lines down a deep tunnel that was dug beneath the school playground for our protection during an Air-Raid. By Christmas, as nothing much had happened, we were told to leave our gas-mask at home. Of course, in the end those rubber masks were never needed because Hitler probably realized that a gas-attack was bound to fail.

Nothing much happened at first, apart from the blackout, gas-masks and big posters on walls everywhere telling us *"Careless Talk Costs Lives"* and *"Loose Lips Sink Ships"*- obviously there was a great fear of spies in our midst. My generous Aunt saved all her sweet coupons for several weeks in order to buy chocolate for my brother and me at Christmas. My mother cut down her dresses to fit me because we never had any new clothes during the war because of few clothing coupons.

Mother (who had conscientiously started following wartime recipes) made "stewed bananas" for tea one day; but, actually, those bananas were really boiled parsnips covered with banana essence. All wartime recipes used very strange alternatives in place of the real ingredients. We never saw bananas until the war was over as they came from overseas. I remember wartime-recipes called 'Air Raid Soup', 'Mock Goose', 'Carrot Flan', 'Glamorgan Sausages' and 'Woolton Pie' (after Lord Woolton who was the Minister for Food Rationing). There was no meat available, but those improvised recipes kept our hunger at bay.

When whole shopping streets were obliterated during the raids of 1940 and 1941 they were replaced with Nissan huts and open markets with tables. Our mothers were the brave heroes of the Home Front and it was amazing how clever they became in the face of shortages and long food queues. They used powdered eggs, powdered potatoes and powdered milk to replace the real things which were strictly-rationed.

I remember how thrilled my cousin was when she won first prize in a raffle at her work — it was a large onion! This terrible shortage of onions was caused by the German occupation of the Channel Islands which had previously supplied Britain with that essential, tasty vegetable.

In 1940, men came and took away the wrought-iron railings that decorated our front garden. They said the iron would be melted down to build ships. They even took the ancient cannons which had decorated Plymouth Hoe since 1588 — the year that Sir Francis Drake captured them from the Spanish Fleet. However, we were told that even Buckingham Palace lost its iron railings. I remember how our beloved King George VI and his family refused to be evacuated to a safe place outside London because he said he would not be able to look Londoners in the face ever again. Later, when Buckingham Place received several bombs the King said he felt closer to his subjects.

Truly, my most horrid memory about the war is being dragged out of bed after the Air-Raid siren sounded ("Moaning

Minnie" we called it) and then running down the stairs and into the garden to hide in our Anderson shelter. I envied those classmates who had a Morrison shelter which was a large steel table with protective sides that people erected in their basement kitchen and thus they did not have to run outside.

I remember how my brave brother liked to stand on top of the shelter to watch a Spitfire and a German plane engaged in a dog-fight overhead. I think it is the BLACKOUT that stays most vividly· in one's memory — with the occasional loud ominous knock on the door from an ever-watchful Air Raid warden to tell mother there was a chink of light showing through the doorway, or window. We soon learned not to run along the street after dark because lamp-posts do not get out of your way — many people were killed by buses because they moved along the dark streets without lights.

My mother had two cousins who died early in the war due to the black-out. One cousin was walking home late at night after working in a munitions factory and did not see a reversing truck which squashed her against a wall and the other cousin was a young sailor returning to his ship in Swansea docks when he fell off the end of the quay in the darkness. It was said that more people died as a result of the Blackout than were killed by bombs.

My father was very sad when he heard about the sinking of his former ship, the 'Royal Oak', that was anchored in Scapa Flow. Somehow, a German submarine had slipped through naval defences and managed to sink that large warship in its home port. Many sailors on board went down with her.

During those dark winter evenings my mother was busy doing "war-work" by sewing shirts for sailors. By incessant stitching on her old sewing machine (the handle type) after we had gone to bed, she could produce about twenty-five shirts each fortnight. My father worked in the Devonport Naval Dockyard as Police Inspector in charge of security. One night when returning home through the nearby churchyard he had a terrible shock when he saw a white figure walking towards him. It proved to be a baker covered in flour after his night's work, but father never took that short cut again.

I think it was our mothers who were the real heroes of those dark days because they kept the home fires burning and struggled to keep us warm and fed — and they queued for hours in the bitter cold and rain to buy any extra commodities that were not rationed, such as fish. Of course, we were all awaiting the arrival of "the German Hordes and that wicked man" who led them. In school we sang *"There'll Always Be An England"* so many times that it became our national anthem.

Everyone was told to buy National War Bonds to help win the war (but at the end of the war when my mother tried to cash her war bonds they were absolutely worthless). The first bomb attack on Plymouth came in March, 1940, and then in March and April, 1941, until Plymouth became the most heavily-bombed city in England (apart from London). During those attacks on our famous naval port, many historic buildings were destroyed for ever, especially our ancient churches. (Hitler had given orders to his pilots to bomb all churches, thinking it would destroy our faith!)

Between March, 1940, when the bombing started, and the last German attack in April, 1944, my home town of Plymouth suffered 59 bombing raids. The final result was over 2,000 civilians killed; 4,000 severely injured; and 72,000 buildings destroyed. Of course, many bodies were never recovered from the ruins.

It was on March 20th. 1941, that I remember standing in

the city centre to see King George and Queen Elizabeth as they slowly walked amongst us and spoke to people. After our beloved king and queen had toured the city and seen the damage done and spoken words of praise to our brave air-raid wardens and firemen, they boarded their train back to London. It was lucky they left Plymouth at 4 o'clock — because about 2 hours later wave after wave of German bombers entered the skies above us and a rain of death began to pour down on the city below.

That raid lasted four hours — and the enemy came again the next night; and during those two terrible nights in 1941 much of the city centre was destroyed. While Plymouth was being bombed we slept on bunkers inside the tiny Anderson shelter in our back garden. My family survived, but each raid was a long and horrible nightmare. Many Plymouth people lost their lives and countless houses were destroyed. One of the worst tragedies was when a city Hospital was bombed, killing 6 nurses and 23 babies — also, in the Royal Naval Barracks a direct hit killed 80 sailors.

Of course, we were still expected to attend school during the daytime and because many school buildings were destroyed by bombs, children had to share schools and so we only attended for half the day. I consider myself to have been very lucky — in spite of food rationing and bombs I did not starve and was not physically injured.

Plymouth's heart was torn out and mauled — but looking back on it from a distance, I have a sense of pride about the heroism and kindness shown by ordinary people. In spite of the destruction of her many historic buildings, Plymouth's indestructible spirit lived on. When the ancient cathedral of St Andrew's was lying in ruins, a mysterious hand wrote on its wall RE SURGAM ("I WILL RISE AGAIN").

Beneath the light of a full moon, enemy planes would arrive and rain down incendiary bombs to light up the ground beneath and thus enable them to see their targets before unleashing any bombs. My father's cousins who lived in the far west of Cornwall, said they could see a red glow for weeks in the distant sky as Plymouth burned to ashes. My mother's sister was so frightened during one raid that she left her house and ran down the street to join us in our Anderson shelter. I remember how she suddenly said she would have to go back and get her false teeth. "Don't be daft," said my mother, "You don't need your teeth, Hitler's dropping bombs, not sandwiches!"

My best friend and her parents were killed after a direct hit upon their Anderson shelter one night — and the only thing rescued from the rubble was "one finger". Air Raids were not of course restricted to the hours of darkness and one afternoon my piano teacher and her pupil were killed when her house was hit by a landmine. Luckily, I was late for my lesson that day or I would have been killed, too!

One night in March, 1940, a landmine fell into our next-door neighbour's garden, making a huge crater. Fortunately for us it did not explode and on the following day a band of men arrived to defuse it. All over Plymouth disposal squads were at their work, coolly, efficiently and with complete disregard for personal danger as they dealt with so many unexploded bombs. These brave men had one of the most terrifying jobs on earth — and what strong, steady hands and brave hearts they needed.

Sadly, there were occasions when a bomb squad lost their lives during such dangerous work. One squad had removed a heavy landmine from the Hoe and were about to drive it away on a lorry when it exploded. The lorry was blown to pieces and all five men were killed.

When our American cousins arrived in Plymouth near the end of 1943 they were greeted with flowers, kisses and open arms. A million Yanks were stationed in Devon and Cornwall to practise for the invasion of Hitler's Europe — although we did not know the purpose of their arrival at the time. At last, Britain was no longer alone in her fight for freedom against the armies of Germany, Italy and Japan — the mighty United States of America had now joined us in the battle against Hitler's evil ambitions.

Those young Yanks had such an easy-going charm and happy life-style which appealed to the young people of England who enjoyed their music, their conversation, their chewing gum and nylon stockings. Kids would follow them along the street asking, "Got any gum, chum?" — and after a bombing raid, those kind American soldiers could be seen working with bulldozers and trucks to rescue folks from ruined buildings, as well as cleaning up the mess and clearing the roads. Plymouth folks felt they were no longer fighting their battles alone.

Our young women were attracted to those smartly-uniformed young men and soon the air was ringing to the sounds of the jitterbug as young couples gaily danced to this lively music. Of course, girls also loved those gifts of nylon stockings and sweets — in return for certain favours, of course. However, it was on June 6th. in 1944 that we woke up to a city that was suddenly silent and empty of soldiers — of course, we did not know that all those Yanks had gone quietly into the night upon their landing crafts across the Channel to the beaches of Normandy. Sadly, thousands of them were mown down by German machine-guns as they waded ashore on Omaha beach.

I think that war changed the role of women for ever

because it took them out of the house — away from the title of simply being a "wife and mother". They took on all the jobs that had been done by men before — working on farms, delivering the post, bus drivers and conductors, working in factories, even flying planes. Yes, women kept the home fires burning and brought victory on the Home front.

I think my most vivid memory of the war was the courage with which people carried on their ordinary lives — always showing a kindness to one another -friend, or stranger — that will never be recaptured in modern times.

The way in which we had to live throughout the Blitz must be unimaginable to people of post-war generations. The official total figure by the end of the war for civilians killed in Great Britain was 60,595 (nearly 70,000) — there were 86,182 (over 86,000) seriously injured and 150,833 (almost 160,000) slightly injured.

Of course, London as Britain's capital city was the main target for Hitler's hatred and the damage to that place was terrible. London had those terrible V1 and V2 Rockets (flying bombs) towards the end of the war and they say if the Germans had invented them six months sooner it could have changed the outcome — about 5,000 Londoners were killed by those pilotless bombs. However, the Germans complained when our brave Air Force retaliated and bombed its cities because they did not like a taste of their own medicine, did they? Thanks to the help of American bombers we know how badly the German cities suffered — but the Germans should blame that evil man called Adolf Hitler who led them into a terrible war and they blindly followed him, so they can only blame themselves!

The Duke of Cornwall

THE DUCHY OF CORNWALL

The Duchy of Cornwall refers not to the entire county, but only to the estates owned by the Duke of Cornwall; mainly farms, woodlands and a few castles. The title also refers to the many Duchy estates and properties outside Cornwall.

The Duchy was created by Edward III as an estate for the eldest son of the monarch. In 1337 Edward the Black Prince rode to Launceston castle to be proclaimed the first Duke of Cornwall and to meet his tenants.

As the eldest son of the monarch Prince Charles is the current Duke of Cornwall

HRH Prince Charles became Duke of Cornwall at the age of four, on his mother's accession to the throne. In 1973 he too travelled to Launceston to be proclaimed the 24th Duke and to meet his tenants. He also received his feudal dues, an extraordinary collection of items which included a pair of white gloves, a brace of greyhounds, a pound each of pepper and the herb cummin, a bow de 'arburne, a pair of gilt spurs, 100 specially struck silver shillings, a carriage of wood to be delivered daily and a salmon spear.

The Prince receives nothing from the Civil List, his only income being derived from the Duchy. As chairman of the Prince's Council, he is ultimately responsible for the management of some 128,000 acres of land comprising almost 200 farms, leased to tenant farmers, and 2,400 acres of woodlands, all of which play an important role in Cornwall's economy. The Duke takes a personal interest in the estate's management, making frequent visits to its woodlands, farms, sawmills and nurseries, even occasionally lending a hand with the milking of cows, planting of crops and building of walls.

CONCLUSION

These stories have been about Cornish life, manners, superstitions and customs, with reference often to my own mining ancestors and their fate.

Obviously, those people of Old Cornwall were very hard workers and they certainly knew what it was like to grow up in big families when money was scarce — and in the days long before electricity, or piped water, arrived in outlying hamlets and villages.

Dentists, doctors and hospitals were unknown to them because the working-classes could not afford such luxuries.

Today, the Duchy of Cornwall has been transformed into a Tourist Mecca and the road-bridge across the River Tamar is often so crowded during the summer months that queues of cars stretch for two or three miles on the Devonshire side.

Sadly, cottages and houses are purchased by wealthy foreigners to be used solely as holiday accommodation; consequently, the natives can no longer afford to live in the villages where their ancestors had lived for centuries before them.

It is almost impossible these days to hear a genuine Cornish dialect spoken in the county, however hard one listens.

The mining of tin and copper is now finished after thousands of years; and the little fishing boats once used to catch pilchards can be hired to convey tourists around the coast.

The old folks would not recognize this modern Cornwall, nor the villages where they lived all their lives. Unlike drivers of modern motor cars, the old folks never wandered away from the places where they were born.

They never had cinemas, wireless, cheap newspapers, or football matches, so they made their own amusements — yet their lives were never dull.

As for the Cornish language, no one knows how to speak it any more. There are written mottoes to be found — such as "Guare wheag yu guare teag" ("Gentle play is handsome play") — but who can pronounce these words?

Still, perhaps this little book will give the reader some insight, however small, into the Cornwall of long ago. Today, we can travel easily and unhurriedly through life. We enjoy luxuries and plenty of leisure time and have many opportunities to choose our road ahead.

But those old folks had endurance which enabled them to survive the many hazards surrounding their lives. They possessed tenacity which enabled them to forge a way along the hard path ahead.

Above all else, they were generous to those who accompanied them on that perilous journey through fife.

Historical Facts of Cornwall

1. The fungus (phytophthora infestans) was attacking potato crops in Cornwall about 1848 before it arrived in Ireland.
2. In the 1850's two-thirds of the world's copper was produced in the Camborne-Redruth area by 350 mines employing 50,000 underground workers.
3. When the Cornish mines closed down because cheaper deposits of tin and copper were discovered overseas, miners and their families were forced to emigrate overseas (to America, Mexico, Australia, Canada, or South Africa).
4. In the 4th. Century Saint Sampson came from Wales and christianised a stone pillar being worshipped by the heathen Celts by carving a cross on its side.
5. Cornwall has over 4,000 years of history — of these 2,500 are pagan and only 1,500 Christian.
6. In the year 1850 no less than 27,000 hogsheads of pilchards (2,400 fish make a hogshead) were caught off Cornwall and sold to foreign markets in Spain, France and Italy which were Roman Catholic countries.
7. The old folks were very superstitious and believed it was unlucky to have holly in the house, but lucky to have mistletoe which warded off evil spirits. They believed it was unlucky to whistle underground and around the house; to work on New Year's day and Midsummer's day; to spill salt on the table; to cross knives; or to put new shoes on the table. But they believed

horse-shoes were lucky because Evil Spirits can only travel in unbroken circles.
8. Beginning in 1859, the Cornwall railway took 17 years to build and involved 42 timber viaducts.

www.ingramcontent.com/pod-product-compliance
Lightning Source LLC
Chambersburg PA
CBHW042112100526
44587CB00025B/4028